Emotional Well-being for Children with Special Educational Needs and Disabilities

A Lucky Duck Book

Gail Bailey

Emotional Well-being for Children with Special Educational Needs and Disabilities

A Guide for Practitioners

Los Angeles | London | New Delhi
Singapore | Washington DC

Los Angeles | London | New Delhi
Singapore | Washington DC

SAGE Publications Ltd
1 Oliver's Yard
55 City Road
London EC1Y 1SP

SAGE Publications Inc.
2455 Teller Road
Thousand Oaks, California 91320

SAGE Publications India Pvt Ltd
B 1/I 1 Mohan Cooperative Industrial Area
Mathura Road
New Delhi 110 044

SAGE Publications Asia-Pacific Pte Ltd
3 Church Street
#10-04 Samsung Hub
Singapore 049483

Editor: Miriam Davey
Production editor: Thea Watson
Copyeditor: Sarah Bury
Proofreader: Jill Birch
Indexer: Anne Solamito
Marketing manager: Lorna Patkai
Cover design: Wendy Scott
Typeset by: C&M Digitals (P) Ltd, Chennai, India
Printed by: Replika Press Pvt Ltd, India

Library of Congress Control Number: 2011945329

British Library Cataloguing in Publication data

A catalogue record for this book is available from the British Library

ISBN 978-1-4462-0159-6
ISBN 978-1-4462-0160-2 (pbk)

Contents

List of Figures and Tables

Figure

Tables

About the Author

Dr. Gail Bailey is a Child Psychology Consultant based in West Wales. She specialises in the emotional well-being of children and young people with special educational needs and disabilities, delivering training to local authorities and other organisations.

Gail is also an elected member of the Editorial Board of *Educational Psychology in Practice*, the Journal of the Association of Educational Psychologists and is an accredited Realise 2 Strengths Practitioner. She is currently acting as consultant to the Learning Support Division of the Welsh Government for young people with ALND undergoing transition to adult services.

She completed her Doctorate in Educational Psychology at University College London on the Emotional Well-being of Children and Young People with Visual Impairments and is now a visiting lecturer there. She has presented papers on her research nationally and for the International School Psychology Association in Finland, 2007, and Dublin, 2010.

As an applied positive psychologist, Gail is devoted to enabling front-line practitioners to help children, young people and their families to lead fulfilled lives.

Acknowledgements

As a person with a severe sight impairment who has had her own emotional well-being challenged at times, especially in the early days of coming to terms with the implications for self and others, I'd like to thank my own teacher, Dr Seán Cameron, for reminding me of my strengths.

He was the person who introduced me to the concepts of Positive Psychology and post-traumatic growth, both of which have added to the applications of my research and practice and ultimately to this book.

I must also thank the children and their families, too many to mention, who have constantly impressed me with their zest for life, application to problem-solving and optimism in the face of their challenges. They have helped me to help other families and teachers who have had periods of real adversity too.

Throughout this book there are case studies designed to help practitioners relate the approach to people they work with. You may read one and think that it is identical to a child that you know, but please be assured that all cases, while based on observations of practice, are not based on individual children. Each is an assimilation of knowledge and experience in working with a range of children over many years.

I would like to thank Miriam Davey and Alex Molineux, Assistant Editors at Sage Publications, for their encouragement and enthusiasm about this project.

Finally, thank you to my family, Rowan, Tanya, Arthur and Sandra for all their positive emotional support during the research and writing of this book.

Foreword

An invasion of armies can be resisted, but not an idea whose time has come. (Victor Hugo, *L'histoire d'un Crime*, 1877)

The apparently unstoppable advance of the Positive Psychology movement vividly illustrates the accuracy of Victor Hugo's quotation and it does not require an in-depth analysis to uncover the reasons why ... The Positive Psychology stance appeals just as much to the experienced practitioner as it does to the enthusiastic trainee! It offers a different slant on the discipline of Psychology by focusing on building up human strengths and well-being and offers both supporting professionals, such as applied psychologists, and direct contact professionals, such as teachers, an alternative to spending all their efforts helping people to patch up their problems.

Positive Psychology is the scientific study of optimal human functioning and flourishing. In short, it focuses on the possibilities which exist when we focus on what is right in life. However, this does not involve its adherents in the permanent wearing of rose-coloured spectacles. Indeed, the Positive Psychology movement began with the premise that for over a century applied psychologists have provided important answers to many human problems. So, this approach accepts that people's existing problems do need to be tackled but at the same time a Positive Psychology perspective also recognises the power of Psychology as a positive force for proactive intervention and for building up (as opposed to patching up) human development.

Despite its obvious application to teaching and learning, surprisingly little research has been reported on its use in school settings, so what is so refreshing about Gail Bailey's book is that it provides a practical base for applying Positive Psychology in the classroom. This is a book which contains opportunities for teachers of children and young people with and without special educational needs, to revitalise their everyday work with creative suggestions for enhancing learning.

The possibilities which could be created by such opportunities include a more positive and optimistic learning atmosphere in the classroom and an increase in pupil/student competence, connectedness and confidence. After all, it is likely to be easier for teachers, parents and carers to help children and young people build up their strengths than to spend most of their time correcting their weaknesses!

Dr Seán Cameron

Co-director of the Continuing Professional Development Doctorate in Educational Psychology at University College London.

Introduction

Why is This Book Needed?

In the course of my work as an educational psychologist over the years, I have been concerned by children and young people with special educational needs and disabilities (CYPSEND) who are reported by their teachers or social workers or parents to be in need of emotional support. Many of these children never get to see a psychologist or counsellor, either because of the stigma attached to seeing a mental health professional or because their parents are unable to afford the time or money to get them to appointments. I am also aware that resources that put in place trained professionals like myself are in restricted supply. This book is written with these children in mind and aims to support those who know them best in their endeavours to improve the child or young person's quality of life. The primary intention is preventative: that by sharing current knowledge of factors supportive of emotional well-being, practitioners may consider whether or not such factors are in place and thereby take action to offset psychological distress. More importantly, however, the book is intended to actively promote emotional well-being in this group of vulnerable children and young people.

We are all aware of the importance of early intervention and this book also stresses the barriers to social and emotional development that may present on account of a child's special educational needs or disability. In doing so, it may enable practitioners and parents to engage in approaches that compensate for these barriers. For example, parents and practitioners working with a two-year old child who has severe sight impairment may need to explain and demonstrate the play function of a ball. They need to explicitly explain verbally what a ball game means to others where a child is unable to see for themselves and how much fun it is to pass a ball from one person to another. Such partnerships are encouraged in order to address parental need too. Often parents are at a loss as to how to help their child with a special educational need or disability (SEND) which in turn may cause them distress. The book acknowledges the pain that some parents experience in relation to supporting their child with SEND. It provides a photocopiable chapter especially for sharing the approach taken with parents. By providing parents with clear, objective information about a child's SEND and encouraging the recognition of capabilities, the practitioner can support the parent in their own adjustment process. In turn, this may help the parent to support their child at a practical level as well as helping them to be emotionally available for their child.

This book considers emotional well-being in the context of the reasonable adjustments that a school or community may make to help remove the barriers to full participation in school and life experiences. It does so by presenting research evidence based on factors supporting optimal adjustment following acquired physical disability and is rooted in the Positive Psychology and resilience literature. Little is published about the implications of disability for children's emotional well-being, let alone on strategies that front-line practitioners can apply to actively promote emotional well-being. This book aims to start to address this gap.

Background to the Book

The inspiration for the book is based on the author's research at University College London, which explored the emotional well-being of children and young people with visual impairments (Bailey, 2011). The emotional well-being and motivation of children and young people with visual impairments (CYPVI) is a common concern among professionals working with them. However, there was a dearth of educational psychology literature relating to the emotional well-being of these children, as discovered through a review of the international literature. With a view to addressing this, the research explored the attributions of young people about factors supporting adjustment following sight loss.

The study involved 26 children and young people of 11–15 years of age, of mixed ethnicity and gender and attending school in nine local authorities across the North East of England. Those fitting the selection criteria completed a focused and semi-structured interview, which was designed to elicit their self-reported strengths and their views on approaches that may be useful to children and young people adjusting to sight loss.

The research questions were based on factors observed in CYPVI following sight loss and that fitted into a framework based on self-determination theory (Ryan and Deci, 2000) and a model of optimal adjustment following physical disability (Elliot et al., 2002). They also sought to examine whether there were particular strengths associated with CYPVI.

Findings indicated support for the use of the two theories in this population as well as the presence of particular strengths, although a significant number of weaknesses were also revealed, compared to the scores demonstrated in a fully sighted population, and indicated a need to monitor the child's perceptions of personal skills and qualities following a diagnosis of sight loss. Frameworks were developed as tools for exploring whether certain protective factors are present in the young person's context and to signpost important components of their personal action plans.

As well as identifying factors important at an individual level, the approach taken examined the factors that were important for consideration at family, peer group and whole-school level, and has been used to devise training programmes for specialist practitioners working in the field. The approach is relevant to a multi-agency approach and has been welcomed for use more widely in the training of school counsellors in Wales. The framework promotes the use of instrumental support as well as affective or emotional support. Figure 0.1 illustrates measures that may be implemented to support emotional well-being at individual, family and school level to give you a flavour of the holistic approach to emotional well-being that this book espouses.

	Autonomy, e.g. the ability to access print independently	Competence, e.g. ability to keep pace with peers	Relatedness, e.g. participation in school and other extra-curricular activities
Individual level	The timely provision of low vision assessment, aids and training or Braille provision.	Understanding one's eye condition and its implications. Using technology effectively.	Emotional support through the adjustment phase, e.g. development of self-advocacy skills.
Family level	Visual awareness training in mobility and low vision aids to encourage independence and positive social support.	Joint training, e.g. learning how to guide effectively, especially in unfamiliar locations. Knowing the implications of the child's sight loss to enable effective communication of needs.	Emotional support and advice through the grief process (and help to develop coping strategies during the adjustment phase). Support in overcoming ambivalence about the future.
Community/ School system level	The removal of barriers to participation. Modifications to allow the CYPVI to flourish.	Effective educational provision (across the lifespan). Access to work entitlements, etc.	Inclusive provision of leisure services across the lifespan to offset anxiety and the risk of depression. Psycho-social aspects, visual awareness training for peer group and school staff.

Figure 0.1   A taxonomy outlining measures supportive of emotional well-being in children and young people with visual impairments (from Bailey, 2011: 55)

What Does this Book Do?

In Part 1, the reader will be presented with an understanding of the reasons why children and young people with special educational needs and disabilities are at risk of developing mental health problems.

The reader is introduced to the practical application of self-determination theory and research. In particular, it provides a framework with which to understand the importance of autonomy, competence and belonging for the emotional well-being and motivation of children and young people with SEND. As part of this approach, the reader is encouraged to consider the impact of caring styles on outcomes for CYPSEND. Managers may find the approach useful in supporting the delivery of empathic as opposed to sympathetic support.

As well as providing supportive caring styles, the reader is presented with the importance of providing the right social environment for the CYPSEND. Inclusion is a two-way process and awareness-raising about the implications of a child's condition by peers and other adults is important if a child is to be accepted rather than assimilated into a 'non-disabled' social environment.

The reader is introduced to a model of optimal adjustment following acquired physical disability. This is a useful tool for encouraging a systemic response to helping the child, rather than solely expecting a child to develop coping strategies that may be outside their control. For example, it encourages an 'I can do' approach by ensuring that everyone around the child challenges negative thinking and actively works at a multi-agency level to replace lost skills or discover new ones (such as the use of technology). This is done through the use of a self-assessment tool to explore protective factors in the child's life that may be apparent or not, and signposting to the chapters on assessment (Part 2) and action planning (Part 3).

It is hoped that when considering the child's needs, the reader will also develop their understanding of the implication of other physical factors, such as pain and fatigue, for the CYPSEND's emotional well-being.

As part of the Positive Psychological approach taken, the reader is encouraged to understand the significance of recognising the enduring personal qualities of CYPSEND. The purpose behind this is to promote the child's sense of personal control over their situation and to enhance their capability to problem-solve and accomplish the goals set.

The book is also intended to help the reader to develop their understanding of the importance of developmental factors and change for the child. The CYPSEND is growing and developing constantly and interacts with changing environments, particularly when they move house or school. While these changes may bring about opportunities or challenges, external factors, such as advances in medical research or technology, may bring new hope to a family's situation.

In the summary section, a flowchart is provided as a review tool of a possible process for implementation. It makes reference to the appendices of resources, which have also been included for practitioners to use.

The book is written for front-line practitioners who work directly with children, including teachers and teaching assistants, youth workers and social care providers, school counsellors and applied psychologists. Trainee teachers and educational psychologists will find Part 1 useful as an academic introduction to the psychological variables influencing the adjustment of children with SEND, while policy-makers and special needs co-ordinators (SENCOs) may find Chapter 4 onwards useful as a resource for assessing need and sharing resources with front-line practitioners and parents.

Over the years of delivering training in this area, I began to use the term 'systemic optimism' to reflect the child's need to be supported by adults and peers who can help them direct their efforts towards positive change for the future. Knowing that children value the people around them being positive about the future strengthened my decision to share the approach through this book. I hope that the book will enable you to apply 'systemic optimism' confidently and help children to apply strengths and qualities that may otherwise be overlooked.

Part 1
A Model for Classroom Practitioners

1

Emotional Well-being and Children and Young People with Special Educational Needs and Disabilities

Chapter overview

This chapter looks at why children and young people with SEND are at risk of developing mental health problems, and examines how self-determination theory and research can help us to proactively promote the emotional well-being of children and young people with SEND. It defines the terms 'emotional well-being' and 'emotional literacy'.

Key phrases

Emotional literacy; emotional well-being; interactive factors framework; Positive Psychology; self-determination theory

Barriers to Happiness

The emotional well-being (EWB) of children with special educational needs or disabilities (SEND) is a concern of many practitioners working with them. Those with disabilities are at greater risk of developing mental health difficulties than their non-disabled peers. A recent survey of children and adolescents in England, Scotland and Wales, conducted for the Office for National Statistics, showed that children with a mental disorder are three times more likely than those without to have officially recognised special educational needs (49% compared with 15%). The survey also showed that 40% of those who had been issued a Statement of special educational need (SEN) had a mental health disorder (Office for National Statistics, 1999). This fact is concerning but one must remember that the majority of children with SEND enjoy emotional well-being.

The current model of SEN has been based on a deficit model of disability and this has brought limitations in the way that some professionals have interpreted the needs of these children and the way that we provide for them. There has been a tendency for practitioners to focus on the difficulties or existing needs that the child has. This book will show how a proactive approach to EWB in this group of children may improve the effectiveness of their provision. By introducing the latest theories underpinning emotional well-being, performance at whole-class and school level may be improved.

An international conference on the 'science of well-being' was held at the Royal Society in November 2003. In the opening address, Felicia Huppert defined 'well-being as any positive and sustainable state which allows individuals, communities and nations to thrive and flourish' (Huppert et al., 2004). This definition highlights how the individual is part of a wider system and that it is a dynamic state that enables people to thrive (or not). In recent years, the attention to positive life experiences has been motivated by the idea that social science, psychology and medicine have traditionally centred on how human shortcomings can be corrected and that it is time to learn from what works rather than from what does not. A range of characteristics are required for individuals to 'thrive and flourish'. These include positive emotions, engagement and interest, meaning and life purpose, positive relationships, self-esteem, self-determination, vitality, optimism, and resilience (Huppert and So, 2009). The Positive Psychology movement of the twenty-first century is growing in momentum (e.g. Seligman, 2011), and sits well alongside changing perceptions of what it is to be disabled and what rights to expect:

Article 23 of the UN Convention on the Rights of the Child (1989) concerns the rights of children with disabilities:

1 States Parties recognize that a mentally or physically disabled child should enjoy a full and decent life, in conditions which ensure dignity, promote self-reliance and facilitate the child's active participation in the community.

This UNCRC article inadvertently supports the role of self-determination theory in the promotion of emotional well-being. Those who work with or have children with SEND will no doubt recognise the importance of promoting a child's independence, particularly in the transition to adulthood. However, until recently an evidence base to support the processes that can contribute to confidence and the ability to be self-determined has been elusive or inaccessible to front-line practitioners. Self-determination theory, put forward by Ryan and Deci (2000), holds that autonomy, competence and relatedness (or inclusion/belonging) are needs that must be met if one is to experience positive emotional well-being and motivation. In this book, I aim to demonstrate that by understanding the implications of children's disabilities on autonomy, competence and relatedness, classroom practitioners can effectively promote emotional well-being and motivation (see Figure 1.1).

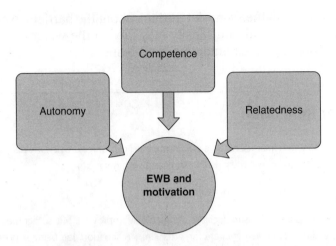

Figure 1.1   Self-determination and emotional well-being (adapted from Ryan and Deci, 2000)

Case Study: Cassie

Cassie (6) met her developmental milestones as expected by her parents until the age of 5 when she developed meningitis, or inflammation of the brain, during the flu season. Her parents were devastated to learn that their daughter acquired profound loss of hearing and epilepsy as a result. Her mother's reaction was 'if only this had happened to me instead of her' as she struggled to come to terms with her child's loss of skills. It seemed that, overnight, Cassie lost her ability to follow instructions and to learn to read, to feed herself confidently and to relate to her friends.

Observations

The implications of the illness mean that Cassie's autonomy, competence and relatedness were affected. The impact of this was a loss of self-confidence and this was a threat to her emotional well-being and motivation. Without the right sort of support to optimise the use of her other skills and other effective support, the limitations would persist. Cassie's mother responded with a guilt reaction and needed emotional support through the period of adjustment to help her learn about the new ways of supporting her daughter and to deal with the uncertinty about the future.

Later in the book, I highlight the implications of different types of disability for functioning in the three areas. The case study highlights how important it is to recognise the parents' needs through the adverse period in order that they may help their child. Throughout this book we will be considering the emotional needs of the child and strategies at an individual, family and school or community level. This is intended to enable practitioners to proactively support EWB in children with disabilities and to help them to work in a child-centred way with other agencies and parents.

In order to further set the scene, let us think about the barriers to participation that a young person with a disability may face in the wider community and how it may impact on their emotional well-being.

Point for Reflection

Joe, a 14-year-old wheelchair user: 'I love swimming but I can only go when my dad comes to visit as it is embarrassing to go into the girls' changing area with my mum.'

What barriers prevent Joe from going swimming?

Physical access to play and leisure facilities are gradually improving, but sometimes the psycho-social aspects and dignity elements are forgotten. In this situation, Joe being exposed to a girls' changing area is embarrassing for him and others around him. Another barrier may be that he is dependent on his immediate family to take part in activities that non-disabled people take for granted. The scenario begs the question: *Why is Joe so dependent on his mum? Why doesn't he have friends who can accompany him when he goes swimming?*

Another barrier is that some children and young people with SEND have fewer opportunities to socialise outside the school setting and may not have had the opportunity to develop and practise the social skills to sustain trusting friendships which would make participation in leisure more possible. For such children, their social and emotional development is an important factor in participation, and the time they spend in school is a valuable opportunity to maximise this aspect of their development.

What is Emotional Literacy?

Interest in developing social and emotional literacy at all levels has grown in recent years. A number of texts aimed at school practitioners are now available and the variety of these reflects a growing interest and demand for information on the subject. For the purposes of this book, the following working definition of emotional literacy will be applied:

> ... the ability to understand ourselves and other people, and in particular, to be aware of, understand and use information about the emotional states of ourselves and others with competence. It includes the ability to understand, express and manage our own emotions, and to respond to the emotions of others, in ways that are helpful to ourselves and others. (Weare, 2004: 2)

I like this definition as it is based on a sound evidence base (the robust research underpinning emotional intelligence, e.g. Salovey and Sluyter, 1997) and reflects what the classroom practitioner perceives as emotional literacy – a set of abilities or skills that can be taught.

Why Emotional Well-being?

While 'emotional literacy' is the main term of reference in this area in the UK, the term 'emotional well-being' has been chosen to reflect the author's preferred holistic and interactive perspective. A disadvantage of the term 'emotional literacy' is that it focuses attention on an individual's capacity or set of abilities. In my view, it is just as important to take into account environmental, management, biological, cognitive and behavioural factors underpinning emotional and social well-being. It also doesn't take into account personality traits or variations in well-being from hour to hour or day to day. Emotional well-being, however, reflects a person's state as dependent on their environment and is less controversial than terms such as 'mental health', which is stigmatising. It is understood in social, educational and health contexts, and the term implies that it is the responsibility of everyone, including parents, students and a range of professionals, and not just that of health departments.

We know that the social and emotional development of a child is a contributing factor to emotional well-being. We are all aware of children with poor social skills who are unhappy in school! In this book we will consider how the implications of different disabilities may impact on social and emotional development as well as EWB. For example, a child who has been diagnosed with an Autistic Spectrum Disorder (ASD) will have impaired social cognition and will therefore have difficulty in learning social rules. This in turn may lead to isolation or challenging behaviour, which in turn impacts on their emotional well-being.

Point for Practice

It is important to mention here that not every child who has a special educational need or disability has delayed social and emotional development or poor emotional well-being. Much depends on their early upbringing, socio-economic factors, character, opportunities and good teaching! A lot of what I have learned about EWB and SEND has been from the optimistic outlook of these children and their parents.

Removing Constraints to Emotional Well-being

By considering EWB rather than a child's set of emotional competencies alone, it allows us to examine the many factors outside the control of a child that may be addressed. The model described in this book introduces strategies to proactively promote emotional well-being. Although this book is about a serious topic, it aims to imbue the reader with an optimistic outlook for the future and allow them to feel confident as practitioners about how they can contribute to the emotional well-being of children and young people with SEND.

Think of the things that make you happy: maybe it's a walk by the sea, going out for a night with your mates, getting a good result in work, having your potential recognised or any number of simple pleasures that contribute to our state of well-being at any one point in time. Imagine what life would be like if you were unable to take part in the activities that you have chosen. For some children with additional needs and disabilities, there are barriers to being able to take part in a range of activities that most of us take for granted.

The Mental Health Foundation, a charity devoted to improving the lives of those with mental health problems or learning disabilities, publishes on its website (www.mentalhealth.org.uk/) a list of activities that one can do to help promote good mental health:

1 Talking about your feelings
2 Keeping active
3 Eating well
4 Drinking sensibly
5 Keeping in touch with friends and loved ones
6 Asking for help when you need it
7 Taking a break
8 Doing something you're good at and enjoy
9 Accepting who you are
10 Caring for others.

Point for Reflection

Which of these activities would be difficult if you were a young person with severe and complex medical needs? How would you feel, knowing that you are unable to take part or that you can take part with a lot of assistance and forward planning? How can schools help to promote these sorts of activities?

You may recognise potential frustration, anger, sadness and anxiety in your response to the last point. Such feelings are all perfectly natural responses by humans to restrictions to their freedom and to a sense of injustice. If these feelings go unaddressed so that the distress persists over time, they may lead to persistent psychological difficulties such as anxiety disorders and depression. Yet, for some children and young people with disabilities, such needs go unrecognised and their emotional well-being is neglected. In addition to these feelings, there are enduring characteristics or personality traits that a person has that will affect their capacity for coping with such adversity.

Such sobering thoughts are not meant to upset you, but to highlight how there are practical obstacles to emotional health that many take for granted and to highlight the potential for addressing some of the risk factors to EWB by working proactively with others to remove the barriers to potential EWB. As professionals, we can provide children and young people with SEND with the competencies to socialise, access information and work with families and other professionals to provide opportunities to enable these children to lead fulfilled lives.

The following case study may be used to raise awareness in professionals about the impact of a hidden disability or visual impairment. I have used it on numerous occasions with teachers, teaching assistants, mobility officers, specialist teachers, counsellors and psychologists. The message it sends is hard hitting but it is a very good way of getting these issues out into the open and to generate discussion about similar cases.

Case Study: A Morning in the Life of a Teenager with a Hidden Disability

Tom is 11 years old. He lives at home with his mother and little sister (aged 9). He attends a mainstream comprehensive with a resource centre for students with visual impairments. He has to get a special bus to and from his new school (which is a long way from where he lives) and where his old friends go to school now. Tom needs to get up a lot earlier than his sister because of this, but also because it takes him a lot longer to get dressed and organised for school. He often takes the wrong books in for lessons because the colours of some of them are impossible to tell apart. His mother cannot help him with this because she has a full-time job and has little time to support him by checking that he hasn't left a book at home by accident. He is anxious about this because he knows that some teachers will give him a de-merit for not bringing in his homework. Because he is busy double-checking that he has everything and starts to rush, he knocks a glass tumbler flying across the kitchen. His mother gets cross with him, calling him clumsy (she doesn't understand why he can see some things sometimes and not others, AND she is stressed because she will need to clear it up before she can go to work). He leaves the house tired, anxious and frustrated.

When he gets off the bus at school, he has time to 'hang out' on the playing field where he tries to join in with chasing and play-fighting games. However, he sometimes misjudges space and bumps into people unexpectedly or trips over clumps of grass. Some avoid him or call him names. This hurts.

When the bell goes and the pupils go in, he passes someone in the corridor that he thinks he talked to at break yesterday about football. However, as he can't see their face and they don't say anything, he remains quiet. At break, he gets close enough to be fairly certain that it was them after all, but they turn away from him and he thinks they don't want to get to know him. He is insecure about forming new friendships, is losing confidence and feels like withdrawing. What is the point in trying anyway – they probably think that he can't enjoy football matches anymore anyway (he thinks).

(Continued)

The first lesson is craft, design and technology, which he misses because he has to have a braille lesson (like learning to read and write all over again!). He'd rather learn how to use tools etc., so that he can help his dad at the weekend.

At break he tries to get a can of drink from the drinks machine but he cannot follow the instructions or see where to put the money in the slot. He is afraid people will look down on him if he asks for help, so he goes thirsty. Another long, lonely, break.

After break it is music and the class are rehearsing songs for a school concert. Tom is good at singing but cannot follow the words. His supply teacher has forgotten Tom's need to have his words enlarged. Tom feels left out and is too embarrassed to bring this to the attention of the teacher.

Before lunch, he has a maths test and is allowed twice as long to complete it with his portable reader-magnifier. He struggles with the graphs – which he used to be really good at – and is disappointed that he has to go to lunch very late so that he can finish the test (he rushes a bit and doesn't bother to check his work). His motivation is suffering.

Well, you can just imagine what lunchtime must be like for Tom, starting with having to work out what the choices are on the menu today …

Questions

1   Note down the feelings that Tom had through his morning. Are there others that may have been experienced by him?

2   How would Tom see himself in comparison with other children? (Use your empathic understanding or try to think from Tom's point of view.)

3   What are the implications for Tom:

in his relationships with other children?
in other school areas and competencies?
for his self-esteem, independence and motivation?

4   Do any of these implications undermine his emotional well-being?

In the following chapters the reader will be provided with some instrumental (practical) and affective (emotional support) strategies to help offset prolonged psychological distress and in so doing aims to proactively support emotional well-being in children and young people with SEND.

The EWB Agenda in Schools

There is increasing recognition that each classroom practitioner needs to be aware of the barriers to participation in education that exist. All teachers are teachers of children with special educational needs or disabilities. We are inadvertent agents of change in the promotion of the core aims to promote well-being in classrooms and the onus is on delivering better outcomes for our most vulnerable children. This book also aims to tackle emotional well-being in its wider sense and outlines strategies for supporting and enlisting the support of parents and other carers of children and young people with SEND.

In addition to this, the emotional intelligence and literacy movement has transcended the curriculum. In some classrooms, children with disabilities are unintentionally excluded from the implementation of such a curriculum. For example, a child who is visually impaired may not be able to read non-verbal gestures such as facial expressions, and thus will face difficulty in accessing teaching materials aimed at teaching the young child about expressing emotion through drawings or pictures of different facial expressions. In this book, practical examples will be given as to how one might modify teaching materials to address the implications of a range of disabilities and to optimise participation.

On Systemic Optimism

1 Deficit Models Versus the Ecological Perspective

Definitions of special educational needs have traditionally been based on a deficit model, where one considers the extent to which an individual deviates from the normal expectations, e.g. significant difficulties in learning compared to a population of children of the same age. Frederickson and Cline (2009) analyse the two conceptualisations of the nature of these difficulties which have prevailed in the latter quarter of the twentieth century: the focus on individual differences and the focus on environmental demands. These authors conclude that neither conceptualisation is adequate on its own, going on to outline the current support for an interactional analysis of SEN. This book considers approaches that sit within this model.

2 Disability as a Social Construct

'Disability' can be usefully viewed as a social construct that is potentially limiting to individuals when faced with it themselves, especially if they hold negative stereotypes of disability. By determining the positive growth that can occur from trauma and the adversity facing children with SEND, this book aims to challenge people's negative beliefs and to start to effect positive change.

Young people with SEND do not grow up in isolation and a learner's achievement is a result of an interaction between the cognitive skills already held by that person at that point in time and in that social context. A critical aspect of growing up is the borrowing of ideas, language, behaviour or problem-solving through collaborating with family, teacher or peers.

Children quickly acquire roles, values, ways of behaving, and ways of coping with their world, depending on their family culture within the context of the wider social culture. As children get older, the school culture and peer group have an increasing impact on personal outcomes.

This book poses positive as well as problem outcomes following the trauma of 'disablement'. The values and perceptions that adults and young people hold about disablement are critical in shaping positive values and self-perceptions as a person with a special need or disablement. If society holds negative attributions about people with disabilities, we run the risk of passing on these values to people affected. It is therefore important to avoid this in order to protect the person's identity.

Rasmussen et al. (2003) report on the pioneering work of Claude Steele (2000), who has been attempting to identify the contextual variables that affect ethnic minorities, another group which experiences exclusion. According to Steele, the very prospect of being negatively evaluated (e.g. through stereotyping) can lead to lowered performance. His evidence specifies that the decreased performance is not through lack of effort, but that high levels of effort are disrupted by the potential of a negative stereotype. Steele advocates the design of environments for 'identity safety', suggesting that specific guidelines are drawn up to ensure that diversity is respected across environments, thus giving all individuals the opportunity to thrive. We also risk restricting the life experiences of students through our own lowered expectations of what a child or young person with SEND can achieve if we do not actively promote diversity in the environment. Some of the most valued strategies used by my clients have been 'awareness-raising' workshops around the implications of their disability for teachers and peers. Inclusion is not just about a child with SEND being assimilated into a non-disabled world; it is a two-way process that enriches the life experiences and perspectives of all. This can only be achieved by the removal of the barriers of psycho-social aspects such as assumptions about what a disability involves, fear or embarrassment. Therefore, this book calls for a new systemic optimism that offers positive support and encouragement to children and young people challenged by SEND.

Chapters 2 and 3 outline the research background to the approach taken for the benefit of trainee teachers, psychologists, counsellors and youth workers who need the background evidence for the approach taken. However, as the book progresses, the approach taken emphasises the application of these ideas to practice. For now, the main implications for practice are:

- children and young people with SEND are at greater risk of developing prolonged psychological distress than their non-disabled peers;
- they may also be at risk of developing delays in social and emotional development due to restrictions in their experiences or participation;

- emotional literacy may need to be addressed as well as emotional well-being;
- promoting emotional well-being is about helping the child to develop age-appropriate social and emotional skills, providing emotional support *and* promoting autonomy, competence and belonging;
- it is important to work at an individual, child and school/community level to offset barriers to EWB in children and young people with SEND.

Summary

In this chapter we have:

- discussed the rationale for a book specifically on the EWB of children and young people with SEND;
- covered the distinction between emotional literacy and emotional well-being, and how they interact;
- examined the social model of disability and how it supports the well-being of the child in their context;
- started to think about self-determination theory and implications for classroom practice.

2
Emotional Well-being and Disability

Chapter overview

In this chapter we will look at the background to the increased risk of mental health problems and social exclusion in children with SEND. This will support the position that EWB is becoming increasingly important to young people's life chances and that there is a growing urgency in the need to tackle EWB. If we want to give all individuals an equal start in life, and to ensure the emotional and mental health of the next generation, youth policy should explicitly focus on developing the emotional well-being of young people, including those with SEND.

Concepts of special educational needs in the twenty-first century will also be examined. The inter-locking theoretical models, which may offer an explanation for what is happening when students maintain or regain optimal experiences, are discussed.

An evaluation of this knowledge base is used to build a model explaining the rationale.

Key phrases

Attribution theory; identity; inclusion; learned helplessness and depression; learned optimism; locus of control; post-traumatic growth; protective factors; resilience; risk factors; self-efficacy; self-worth; social exclusion

Since the Office for National Statistics (ONS) (1999) survey mentioned in Chapter 1, wider research on the mental health of children has reported on how children with disabilities are at greater risk of developing longer term mental health problems and social exclusion than their non-disabled peers (WAG, 2001, 2010; Emerson, 2007). However, their needs are largely overlooked in the emerging policies and practice guidelines issued by government, probably as a result of a relative dearth of research into the area. We will now look at some of the evidence relating to the risk to mental health of children and young people with SEND. Arguments, principles and strategies to minimise the risk and build better outcomes for this vulnerable group by applying Positive Psychology will be introduced.

Risk Factors for Children and Young People with SEND: The Evidence Base

- In an average UK community of 250,000 people, there will be 1,575 children with intellectual disability (Emerson, 2007). Of these, 570 will have an active, diagnosable mental health problem and 330 will have an active diagnosable conduct disorder or challenging behaviour. With one in three children with learning disabilities alone suffering in this way, *what are the implications for being able to provide effective emotional support to address such difficulties?*
- There is a need to take such figures seriously as about 7% of the 0–16 childhood population have a disability and they are the fastest growing group of disabled people – an increase of 65% since 1975.
- Only 4% of children with disabilities currently receive support from social services – another common concern. This causes particular concern at the point of transition as the eligibility criteria for access to adult services varies significantly (figures from Russell, 2008).
- 16–19 year-olds with disabilities are twice as likely as their non-disabled peers to be out of education, training or employment. Pupils with additional needs/disabilities are three times more likely to be permanently excluded than other pupils.

As well as the disappointing statistics above, there are accompanying challenges for parents:

- Rates in diagnosis of developmental disorders such as ADHD, Autistic Spectrum Conditions and anxiety about seeking early diagnosis and the best interventions are increasing. Parents are subject to increased general knowledge about such conditions but limited opportunity for accessible guidance on evidence-based approaches. At a time when they really need to have knowledge and information to help their child, the resources to help them access this information are often elusive.
- There is a similar increase in infants being diagnosed with complex health needs and disabilities. Often a diagnosis is also elusive and the parent struggles to find an understanding of how to meet their child's needs or how to explain the implications of these needs to others, such as teachers and welfare benefits clerks.
- 44% of children with a learning disability have a mother with a past or current mental health problem. This has serious implications for a child with or without a disability, as their parent may not be available emotionally to the child if they have inadequate support themselves. However, raising a child with SEND brings additional stresses, e.g. additional costs and hospital appointments, and can mitigate against the parent's own emotional well-being.

- 38% live in households where no one is employed. Children and young people with SEND are therefore likely to be disadvantaged financially and may have a restricted opportunity for going out as a family or joining in other events and social activities. 33% find it hard to make friends and 44% of parents said they do not receive sufficient support (figures from Emerson, 2007).

Examining such data gives cause for concern as it highlights variables at play in the lives of children with SEND that we can often do little about in a direct way. However, increasingly, professionals are becoming aware of factors that are proven to promote resilience in children who are presented with adversity. One recognised protective factor that practitioners are aware of is the need for a close caring relationship (Newman and Blackburn, 2002), and the social care system has been actively applying this principle for many years now in the provision of services to children in the care system. Applying measures to support such relationships are certainly achievable. Approaches that promote resilience and offset risk factors due to disability are discussed later in the book, as are the core aims of well-being monitors, including the safeguarding of children and young people with SEND.

A challenged sense of identity, social exclusion, loss reactions and a quest for self-efficacy are some of the challenges that the child with SEND may face. This section considers the relevant psychological variables relating to these issues.

The Development of Identity

Vygotsky (1987), and other accounts of his work (e.g. Daniels, 2001), provides some useful examples of conditions influencing compensatory (adaptive) processes which may help to challenge traditional models of disability. There is a case for an interactive approach to the assessment of the needs of a child with additional needs and disabilities.

Vygotsky pointed out that in future we would be ashamed to use the term 'impaired child'. In this book, we deconstruct pathology further by arguing for the need to establish active progress towards this by maximising the learning environment (including the role played by personality and social interaction).

Learned Helplessness and Depression

Seligman's theoretical model of learned helplessness (1975) has provided the explanation for the depression that results from not being in control of a situation and becoming dependent on the support readily offered when a person becomes disabled.

In the absence of skill-orientated interventions aimed at optimal restored independence, e.g. in mobility and daily living skills, young people may become acquiescent and may even accept that the pity that 'helpful' people have towards them is a feeling that they should have themselves. The depression commonly reported, then, may be the result of their own perceived helplessness combined with self-pity reinforced by the attitudes of people around them.

The learned helplessness model certainly offers a plausible explanation for what is going on and has been widely accepted as a theoretical model of depression for many years. However, what are required are evaluated clinical accounts of the problems and interventions to address them, especially those relating to children and young people with disabilities. Imagine the conflict arising in a young person who opts to achieve greater independence again, but who has been cosseted by a loving but over-protective family (as described, for example, in Doss and Hatcher, 1996). There is a need to address the perceptions held by other people in the wider environment – in order to support the young person (and carers, friends and support workers). There are, undoubtedly, examples of families of young people who manage to achieve a balance in the level of support achieved. *What can we learn from these in order to give evidenced guidance to those who wrestle with these issues? What are their observations about other environmental factors?*

The growing literature on 'learned optimism', also led by Martin Seligman, is actively contributing to a culture whereby people may learn how to take life's challenges in their stride by adopting the cognitive behavioural patterns of optimistic people. His books on the subject are bestsellers (e.g. Seligman, 2003) and encourage readers to understand their own explanatory style in order to avoid helplessness and depression.

Key Points:

- Skill-orientated interventions may offset dependency, a lack of control and helplessness.
- Such optimal experiences may offset depression.
- Conflict may arise when others around the person with a disability prefer to sustain dependency.
- More research is needed in this sensitive area.

Attributional Style

Abramson et al. (1978, 1987) reformulated the original learned helplessness model by proposing that people differ in the way that they attribute external or internal causes to events. For example, those with an internal attributional style for success and an external attributional style for failure tend to maintain good levels of self-esteem. Attribution theory and its applications in the educational psychology literature has grown since that time, although there is no research specific to the field of children and young people with disabilities. Miller, Ferguson and Byrne (2000) relate the contribution of Weiner's (1979, 1985) model, which identifies four dimensions of attribution: control, stability, locus and globality.

He has been able to distinguish between pupils who exhibited adaptive mastery-orientated behaviour and another group which demonstrated helpless achievement behaviour by applying this model of differing attributional patterns. They proposed that those students who had successfully adapted following a diagnosis of additional need or disability would attribute their success to internal, mainly stable and controllable causes.

Key Points:

- Self-esteem is protected by internal attributions for success and external attributions for failure.
- Those who adapt well to SEND attribute success to stable, internal and controllable causes.
- Those working with children with SEND may help adaptation by restoring a sense of mastery over their environment.

Self-worth

Self-esteem is central to understanding an individual's adjustment to disability. For example, the lowering of self-esteem following sudden sight loss may be a reaction to the negative sighted stereotypes of the label of visually impaired or blind. Also, a reduced sense of competency may lead to demoralisation, as demonstrated in clinical literature (Figuerido and Frank, 1982).

Self-esteem is associated with an absence of anxiety and depression as well as high feelings of self-efficacy. Some researchers (e.g. Dodds et al.,1991) suggest that self-esteem may be increased by either concentrating on the alleviation of anxiety or depression or by working on increasing the feelings of self-efficacy.

The explanation of the effect of negative stereotyping following labelling sits closely with cognitive theories of attribution and social constructs. The diminished competency leading to demoralisation seems inextricably linked with our understanding of self-efficacy and self-determination.

Key Points:

- Self-esteem is associated with the absence of anxiety and depression.
- Working on the alleviation of anxiety and depression and improving self-efficacy may improve self-worth.
- Improving a child's sense of competency may enhance feelings of self-efficacy and self-worth.

Locus of Control and Self-efficacy

People differ in the extent to which they internalise or externalise perceived control. People with an internal locus of control believe that they can change things whereas those with an external locus of control believe that things are influenced by factors beyond their control. The effect on motivation of internalising that control is to cause them to act whereas the effect of externalising it is to become passive.

Self-efficacy is closely linked to the concept of locus of control. Bandura (1977), for example, emphasised the importance of self-efficacy to achievement motivation. Those with a low sense of self-efficacy will be reluctant to try new tasks because they expect to fail at them, as they feel that they have little control over their situation. Methods of developing self-efficacy have been devised (Weiner, 1979).

Can one assume that one's locus of control, if previously internal, remains unaffected when faced with an adverse factor such as permanent, incurable (and maybe degenerative) conditions? In my opinion, the way in which a diagnosis is imparted to a parent or an individual is critical in determining the locus of control and motivation from that point. The proposition here would be that to be advised of assistive technology in overcoming the diminished functioning resulting from dyslexia, for example, would lead to or retain a normal or internal locus of control.

Self-efficacy is now closely linked with mastery motivation (see the work of Carol Dweck, e.g. Dweck, 2000) and intrinsic motivation.

Key Points:

- Internalising control by enabling a child to engage with their curriculum and other activities can promote active learning rather than passivity.
- Children with low self-efficacy will resist trying new tasks that may lead to failure as they believe they have little control over their success.
- Providing children with alternative means of completing activities or tasks at the point of diagnosis may help to preserve an internal locus of control, a sense of self-efficacy and mastery motivation.

Acceptance and Attitude Towards Disability

The importance of acceptance in the adjustment phase following the onset of a disability may be instrumental in being able to predict whether an individual will benefit from rehabilitation (Linkowski, 1967, 1971 and 1987). Linkowski (1987) found that acceptance of disability correlated with attitudes towards disabled people. In the absence of firsthand knowledge of what it is like to live with an additional need or disability, they turn to the societal attitudes of what it will mean in practice, which is often negative.

Research in the area of rehabilitation is based on an adult population and therefore does not add much to our understanding of the cognitive mechanisms or precursors underlying optimal adjustment in children and young people with SEND, although some of its findings support the need for additional needs being met. Perhaps the most important thing to note here is that it is surprising that there is little mention in the education literature of the importance of the psychological factors affecting children and young people with additional needs and disabilities.

However, factors such as 'controllability' (Weiner, 1979, 1985) seem to be gaining ground in terms of motivation research in general.

Key Points:

- Acceptance of one's disability is linked to one's attitudes and assumptions about disability in others.
- Negative attitudes in society towards disability can impact on the child or parent's ability to accept disability as people form opinions from popular culture or what they have or haven't learned about a condition.
- More research is needed on the impact of stigma on children's adjustment.

Inclusion

'Inclusion' reflects the social model of disability where disability is perceived as a product of the environment, attitudes and institutional practice as the impairment itself (Davis, 2003). It may be argued, then, that by altering attitudes and educational practice, schools can help to reduce barriers to access and participation. However, as we have seen, the situation is even more complex than that, as psychological variables are considered important factors in adjustment to disability and these can result, for example, from changed perceptions of self in response to negative stereotyping in the social environment. As one can no longer separate out the within-child differences and environmental demand, an interactionist perspective is the more accurate position to take at this point in time.

As Frederickson and Cline (2009) note, the interactional position has been advocated in government guidance in the UK for many years:

> The extent to which a learning difficulty hinders a child's development does not depend solely on the nature and severity of that difficulty. Other significant factors include the personal resources and attributes of the child as well as the help and support provided at home and the provision made by the school and the LEA and other statutory and voluntary agencies. A child's Special Educational Needs are thus related both to abilities and to disabilities and to the nature and extent of the interaction of these with his or her environment. (DES, 1989: para.17)

Frederickson and Cline (2009) point out that although the interactional approach is widely advocated, it cannot be assumed that it is widely applied in practice.

Concepts of SEN and Disability

The focus on individual differences was driven by legislation prior to 1981 as the Education Act (1944) emphasised disability of mind or body. This conceptualisation has been criticised on a number of key issues:

- A focus on individual needs is based on untested assumptions. Frederickson and Cline (2009) report Solity (1993), who gives the example that it is often assumed that a child has been provided with appropriate learning opportunities or that the teaching available has been successful with peers but not with the child concerned. Although the evidence to support these assumptions is rarely available, they are not often challenged.
- Social and educational contexts are important and were embodied in the first Code of Practice (1994), e.g. differentiating pupils' work can help them engage with the curriculum.
- Where the educational context contributes to the problem, focusing on the individual will do little to contribute to a more effective context. For example, a school that does not offer awareness-raising about a child's disability to general teaching staff will disadvantage the learner, who lacks the confidence to point out that they cannot access the lessons offered. It may be argued that the educational system is not equally favourable to all children and that it should become flexible to the extent where it can embrace individual variation. As Ainscow (1995) notes, meeting diverse needs should be part of the drive to provide a richer learning environment for all (Frederickson and Cline, 2009).

The other standpoint in the past has focused on environmental demands:

- Different children will respond to the same learning environment in different ways: some resilient and resourceful children will achieve despite poor teaching and, conversely, some children may not respond to the most well-planned and skilled teaching available (Frederickson and Cline, 2009).

- Within-child factors can be influenced by teachers and Frederickson et al. (1991) have indicated a number of interventions that have had powerful effects on raising pupils' self-esteem.
- An exclusive focus on the environment lacks credibility with teachers.

Until recently, deficit models of special educational needs (with a focus on a young person's developmental delay and physical deficits) have informed government policy and educational culture in the UK. As discussed above, concepts of disability are changing to embrace diversity and to consider the child's functioning within the environmental constraints restricting functioning in society.

Developing a Fuller Understanding of Inclusion

Increasingly, researchers are turning to the Positive Psychology literature and changing global perspectives of disability for solutions. For example, Delle Fave and Massimini (2003) refer to the revised International Classification of Functioning, Disability and Health (World Health Organisation, 2001), which conceptualises disablement as a product of interacting personal and environmental conditions. This classification comprises three areas: impairment of physiological or psychological functions; activity limitations; and participation restrictions (i.e. the consequences which interfere with the ability to take up the usual social roles). Their research findings suggest that:

> Physical impairments, rather than preventing development, can help individuals discover new opportunities for optimal experience and can foster personal growth. For this reason, rehabilitation programmes and integration projects should pursue two goals. At the environmental level they should provide meaningful opportunities for social integration. At the individual level, they should focus on the activities subjectively associated with optimal experiences in order to exploit the behavioural flexibility and resource potential of disabled people, promoting their development and their active contribution to culture. (Delle Fave and Massimini, 2003: 134)

These are new and challenging recommendations and the educational literature has yet to incorporate such perspectives, although schools have a planning duty to increase the extent to which disabled students can take a full part in the curriculum of the school.

Recent legislation also strengthens the rights of children with SEND to be educated in mainstream schools. Educational professionals will therefore need to examine and develop strategies for successful inclusion within this changing culture. As well as the removal of barriers to the general curriculum, it is essential that professionals consider ways of removing barriers to participation in the wider social context of the school. In order to do this, the optimising of social and emotional development and EWB is crucial.

Post-traumatic Growth and the 'Disability Paradox'

There is a growing psychological literature on post-traumatic growth and the 'disability paradox'. Articles by Linley (2000) and Linley and Joseph (2003) summarise the growing literature on post-traumatic growth and Positive Psychology. The spirit of this work is to examine the human condition under circumstances where people who have experienced trauma (e.g. ill-health or displacement) have identified benefits which otherwise may not have accrued. An example here is a person who has survived cancer or a heart attack and who has gone on to find new meaning in their life.

Albrecht and Devlieger (1999) have examined this disability paradox: why do many people with serious, long-term disabilities report a good to excellent quality of life when (they hold) many people think they lead an undesirable existence? In a semi-structured interview, 54.3% of respondents reported on this quality of life, confirming the existence of such a paradox. Their analysis of responses reveals that quality of life depends on '[f]inding a balance between body, mind and spirit in the self and on establishing and maintaining a harmonious set of relationships within the person's social context and external environment' (Albrecht and Devlieger, 1999: 977).

Other work by Delle Fave and Massimini (2003) explored the optimal experiences reported by people who had become blind, paraplegic or tetraplegic during adolescence or adulthood. In their findings, 41 out of 45 participants recognised optimal experiences in their current life. (For example, blind people mostly associated flow experiences with reading in Braille, listening to radio and TV and work.)

Self-determination Theory and Application to Educational Policy

My casework and research demonstrates a link between autonomy, competence and relatedness being in place and support for emotional well-being as espoused in self-determination theory (Ryan and Deci, 2000), and helps to justify environmental resources to support these protective factors. ICT, with appropriate training, can promote key skills to support competency and autonomy, and is an example of how instrumental solutions may also remove barriers to participation and underpin EWB. It may even be argued that educational policy that does not provide resources to enable the learner to record their responses as fluently as possible may be undermining the child's emotional well-being, depressing motivation and leading to lower achievement!

Identification of the Personal Growth Factors to Address the Absence of Protective Features

Protective factors based on research may serve as a checklist for the identification or an absence of such protective/supportive factors in a young person's environment (including their personal and social domains). The appropriate steps could then be taken to offset these risk factors and actively promote emotional well-being at child, family, school (peer group and whole-school) levels. In later chapters, checklists to assist with this process are presented for the practitioner to apply within their settings. Most checklists examining children's emotional states are based on research into children's development and the research we have accrued about self-worth, motivation, anxiety or depression. Such checklists may indicate when a child may need to be referred on to a child and mental health team or help us describe the nature of a child's psychological state. However, they do little to inform the frontline practitioner on how to promote the EWB of the child with SEND. The approach that this book takes aims to equip practitioners with the knowledge and skills to proactively promote EWB in children with SEND by putting protective measures in place to offset longer-term distress. They are intended as lists of 'can dos' rather than don'ts and are intended to engender what I call *systemic optimism*. In my research, children highlighted how they appreciate everyone around them being positive about their future and helping to remove the barriers that prevent them being able to take part in their education and other activities. It is our responsibility as members of their immediate environment:

- to ensure that children and young people with SEND are supported and encouraged to reach their full potential;
- to facilitate the child's sense of competence, autonomy, and their sense of belonging, as well as to facilitate full participation wherever possible and thereby promote EWB;
- to promote social and emotional development.

Summary

In this chapter we have:

- examined the statistics relating to disability and mental health and other risk factors;
- looked at the research into the psychological variables influencing adjustment in relation to SEND;
- looked at the prevailing educational models and how they mesh with what needs to be achieved to support the EWB of children with SEND;
- introduced changing perspectives in the twenty-first century.

3

The Evidence Base: The Contribution of Positive Psychology

Chapter overview

We have now seen the psychological concerns that may arise for a young person with a SEN or disability. In this chapter, we will see how positive psychological interventions can help to address such difficulties in order to provide background for the forthcoming practical chapters. Readers will begin to see how front-line practitioners can contribute effectively to such interventions and help offset the emergence of such difficulties.

As seen in the previous chapter, there are a number of issues to be considered when focusing on the individual or their environment. Therefore, it may be more appropriate to use the interactional model.

Happiness research, learned optimism and post-traumatic growth are introduced to the reader, as well as the notion of strengths recognition and development, which also have a role in enhancing capability. We will also examine the potential contribution of a model of optimal adjustment, rooted in the Positive Psychology literature, in an effort to address the complex problems that can arise.

Key phrases

Happiness; learned optimism; optimal adjustment; Positive Psychology; post-traumatic growth; self-determination; strengths

Positive Psychology

As Seligman and Csikszentmihalyi (2000: 5) wrote:

> Psychology has since World War II, become a science largely about healing. It concentrates on repairing damage within a disease model of human functioning. This almost exclusive attention to pathology neglects the fulfilled individual and the thriving community. The aim of

positive psychology is to begin to catalyze a change in the focus of psychology from the pre-occupation with repairing the worst things in life to also building positive qualities.

Further on in the same article, they relate to Albert Camus, the existential novelist who said that the most important question for philosophy was 'why should you not commit suicide?' They explain that one cannot answer that question by just curing depression, as there must be positive reasons for living as well. Applying such arguments, it would seem that important issues in psychology and society have been neglected and that it is essential that we expand our thinking in future.

Moreover (and contentiously), discerning weaknesses in humans in order to 'cure' has led to the practice of labelling – a form of discrimination. As an educational psychologist, one always has a careful judgement to make with parents and professionals about whether or not establishing a diagnosis will enhance a child's life or not. Maybe a focus on people's resources and factors, and the measures needed to protect or support these, will lead to better attitudes towards disability. People may learn 'to see the person rather than the disability'. In the longer term, it may even lead to changed social constructs and possibly to the promotion of a positive 'identity' when faced with the adverse factor of disablement.

Three personality traits have been extensively studied in the field of Positive Psychology. These are: subjective well-being, synonymous with the study of *happiness* (e.g. Diener, 2000); *optimism* (e.g. Seligman, 2003); and *self-determination* (Ryan and Deci, 2000). The other important concept to consider in relation to SEND is the concept of *post-traumatic growth*.

Post-traumatic Growth and Development

As we have seen earlier, some studies point to positive life experiences following the onset of disability (Albrecht and Devlieger, 1999; Delle Fave and Massimini, 2003). These studies have emerged from the fascination that psychologists have with the varying responses to stress and trauma.

Tedeschi, Park and Calhoun (1998) explained that researchers are turning their attention to factors which allow children and adults not only to bounce back from trauma, but to use it as 'a spring board to further individual development or growth':

> Post traumatic growth (PTG) is both a process and an outcome. We see it as developing out of a cognitive process that is initiated to cope with traumatic events that extract an extreme cognitive and emotional toll.

... These traumas call into question the basic assumptions about one's future and how to move toward that future, and therefore produce massive anxiety and psychic pain that is difficult to manage. ... In the face of these losses and confusion they cause some people to rebuild a way of life that is superior to their old one. ... They establish new psychological constructs that incorporate the possibility of such traumas, and better ways of coping with them. (Tedeschi et al., 1998: 2)

Aldwin and Sutton (1998), in the same volume, summarise the resilience literature in relation to children and young people. They report the protective characterstics that resilient children often possess which can help protect them from problems later in life. These characteristics, such as gender, intelligence and an easy-going temperament, together with the quality of their relationships, can contribute to positive adaptation. However, it is more appropriate if one takes a social constructivist perspective, to agree with Rutter (1987), who viewed resilience to stress as a process of interaction between the individual and the environment rather than a fixed personality trait.

Reviewing the literature on the evidence for post-traumatic growth in children, Aldwin and Sutton (1998) explain that self-reports of growth following trauma in children is mainly anecdotal. They called for research that will determine influences such as age and developmental level as well as work defining which aspects of the person develop, e.g. personality, social relationships or mental health. These observations call for the phenomenological appraisal of the processes underway in adaptation. My own research examined such factors as well as patterns of strengths following the adverse factor of visual impairment in children and young people (Bailey, 2011).

An Interactive Perspective

One would predict that a number of interacting factors would emerge in such a complex problem. In order to construct the research proposals for my research, I chose an appropriate model as a starting point for categorising the environmental variables contributing to optimal functioning following acquired physical disability. In agreement with Wright and Lopez (2002), it is important to look closely at the person's strengths and weaknesses as well as the resources and stressors available in the environment. Through further exploration of the Positive Psychology literature, a model of optimal adjustment following acquired physical disability (Elliot et al., 2002) offered a particularly relevant means of considering factors that may be contributing to a phenomenological appraisal process in people who have adjusted to physical disability.

Although the research was also based on research with adults, it considered the enduring characteristics of the individual, the social environment and made allowance for the dynamic continuum over time. Through reviewing the literature for my research, it also became apparent that those who were more outgoing in character were more likely to enlist support from others (and hence sustain inclusion and opportunities for developing competence).

Interactional models best describe this position and a socio-ecological model is used to map out the complex, interacting factors which may contribute to optimal adjustment. This is considered within the Positive Psychology context, whereby one considers that those students who experience personal growth or development will be well placed to inform us of the cognitive behaviours and precursors supporting optimal adjustment.

The Environment and Social Issues

Contributing issues here relate to environmental factors, such as whether an environmental audit has been completed for a wheelchair user (and acted on) at school and/or at home to minimise barriers to learning or other activities. They may also include factors such as continued opportunity for inclusion in the range of school activities (e.g. practical subjects, PE, etc.) as well as extra-curricular activities. Peers' attitudes towards disability and one's own attitude towards disability may also come into this category as they are closely connected with the social environment.

Self-determination needs – competence, autonomy and relatedness – are also relevant here. When these needs are satisfied, enhanced self-motivation and well-being are experienced. These have been placed here as environmental variables to determine the extent to which a young person with a disability will feel competent, autonomous or connected.

The early input of skills acquisition training will support personal growth. For example, assistive technology can maintain competence at reading and writing tasks, a claim which is supported by the research findings of Dodds et al. (1991) and Delle Fave and Massimini (2003).

The Personal System

Personality traits, such as an outgoing personality, secure attachments to significant others and the other types of protective factors, are typical of resilience research and are relevant to the approach taken here. Attributions relating to mastery motivation, self-efficacy and locus of control, as well as those relating to stamina, self-esteem and positive attributions about one's identity, also apply.

There may also be references to an optimistic attitude and optimal experiences, e.g. through the enjoyment of mastering new technology (competence and autonomy are associated with good levels of motivation and emotional well-being). In addition, the hope factor and beliefs held individually are also found in this domain.

The Adverse or Transition Period

The early or prompt introduction of skill acquisition training and practical resources is relevant here as well as the availability of emotional support for the young person and their family. Also, the manner in which the diagnosis is imparted may be included here. For example, whether negative attributions about disability were challenged and whether information about what could be done in terms of restoring or improving functioning was provided or not.

The Cognitive Appraisal and Coping Mechanism Process

Support in accepting one's additional needs, which might include sensitive counselling support, contact with positive role models, information and people who are prepared to challenge negative perceptions, help support the cognitive appraisal process. The degree to which mastery motivation is achieved will also impact on the success of this appraisal process. In Elliot's model (see Figure 3.1), this is described as the phenomenological appraisal process (Elliot et al., 2002).

In Chapter 4, you will find a discussion of a self-report questionnaire (reproduced in full in Appendix 2) representing the influences on optimal adjustment developed from this model. These influences are:

- Enduring characteristics and individual differences;
- Social and environmental factors;
- Physical health;
- The dynamic and developmental continuum.

Enduring Characteristics and Individual Differences

Statements from the self-report questionnaire:

- I have been able to encourage young people with disabilities to express themselves effectively and be assertive when required and be confident enough to ask for help

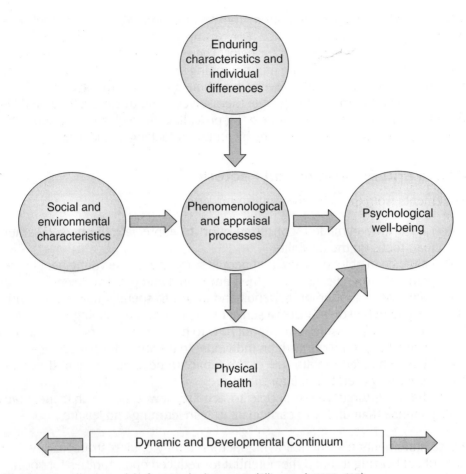

Figure 3.1 Elliot's model of optimal adjustment (Elliot et al., 2002: 687)

- I have encouraged the self-motivation of young people to fully partici-pate in activities of learning
- I have encouraged young people to be hopeful and face the future with confidence and optimism
- I am able to help young people to become objective and help them appre-ciate other people's perspectives
- In the past I have helped young people to overcome barriers through problem-solving
- I have taken steps to ensure that the young person can recognise and make the most of their personal strengths

These statements covered the following aspects of character: locus of control, capacity for adopting a problem-solving approach, the ability to sustain hope and to pursue personal meaningful goals, self-confidence and assertiveness.

The statements were derived from the research on which the model was based and application to practice. For example, let's take the statement on being 'confident enough to ask for help'. The reason for this is that casework indicated that children who are more outgoing are better able to enlist support than those who are more introverted in their approach. To have an indication as to whether the young people themselves think this is useful would be useful for programme planning, e.g. by providing strategies to develop self-advocacy skills where a child is shy by nature or lacking confidence.

Social and Environmental Factors

Statements from the self-report questionnaire:

- I have always made a concerted effort to appreciate the person rather than focus on the disability
- I have been able to ensure that people surrounding the young people are both patient and sensitive to their emotional and physical needs
- I have been encouraging friends and family to spend 'quality time' with the young person to foster a sense of security and belonging
- I do not make assumptions about how to help a young person with a disability. Rather, I work with an individual to discover their needs
- I have changed the attitude of the family to become positive (if necessary) and generate hope for the future
- I have nurtured young people to acquire new skills so that they can enhance their ability to participate fully in learning and leisure

These statements test the following factors: family coping strategies (which are critical bearing in mind the potential for reduced opportunities for socialising, see Elliot et al., 2002), stereotyping, opportunities for self-determined behaviours, the role of feedback from family and peer group regarding 'reading people', and awareness training. They also test factors relating to self-determination theory in the areas of autonomy and relatedness, e.g. having opportunities to socialise outside school/college.

Physical Health

Statements from the self-report questionnaire:

- I have employed a structured approach to help the young person fully understand the implications of their condition on their physical functioning and emotional health
- I have consulted with other professionals to determine whether the condition is stable or not and fully understand the implications
- I fully appreciate not only the prime disability but also other health conditions that may impact upon their well-being

- I have ensured that family and friends are aware that the young person gets sufficient rest to ensure that fatigue does not impact on their behaviour (see Health section – this impacts on all factors supporting EWB)
- I have ensured that the daily routine of the young person contains an active element for physical exercise to overcome anxiety

These statements check out the effects of health in the child's experience as optimal management is important to facilitate independence, real choices, competence and to address self-efficacy issues. Such factors may be related to the adjustment issues commonly associated with referrals for emotional support. The statements relate to low levels of pain, trauma and the stability of the condition, etc.

Dynamic and Developmental Continuum

Statements from the self-report questionnaire:

- I have created a Plan–Do–Check–Act routine to review the young person's progress in the light of their development and disability
- I ensure that as part of my own professional development I am up to date with technological aids that can overcome emotional and disability barriers to the full participation of young people (potential impact on independence, capability and belonging)
- I ensure that I take active measures to keep up to date with medical advances that may contribute solutions towards the management of the disability
- I make an effort to look for interests that excite young people so that I can build real opportunities for active engagement and the pleasure of accomplishment
- I have nurtured young people to acquire new skills so that they can enhance their ability to participate fully in learning and leisure

Statements in this section relate to whether needs are being met appropriately, e.g. the use of technology, the acquisition of new skills with development (e.g. touch typing) and advances in medical treatment (the hope factor). The statements were designed to test the professional's perspective on a sense of competence and self-efficacy, needs that are important according to self-determination theorists and the rehabilitation literature (e.g. Dodds et al., 1991). An important aspect following a diagnosis is the loss of skills and the impact of a sense of loss or grief. It may be argued that any delay in assessment and effective provision may be deleterious to the emotional well-being and motivation of a child with SEND.

With the current onus on partnership working with parents and seeking children's views, the statements devised and tested in my research aim to seek children's views in a fundamental area of special educational needs: the importance of these needs being met. In the assessment section of this book (Part 2), you will therefore find questions related to optimal adjustment. These are organised under the factors that are supportive of self-determination for the child with SEND and are presented from the child's perspective or experiences.

Strengths and Children's Capabilities

Another major contribution that Positive Psychology has to make to the lives of children and young people with SEND is in the area of the recognition of their strengths. Instead of focusing entirely on needs and difficulties being met, it may be argued that there is an important role for identifying the personal skills and qualities that a young person has to help them recognise themselves as a person and to help them recognise and apply their strengths in the future. Such an approach is useful for helping a child to self-advocate, contribute to reviews and to prepare for transition. Again, Seligman (2003) has influenced practice in this area. In the UK, the Centre for Applied Positive Psychology is actively researching strengths coaching (see www.cappeu.com). Chapters 6 and 8 actively apply such strategies in the interests of children with SEND (pp. 57 and 85).

Since starting my research in this area and applying strengths recognition and development to my casework, Martin Seligman has also formulated a model designed to help a child with SEND to flourish – the PERMA model (Seligman, 2011). It neatly sits alongside the main messages in this book:

P = positive emotions

E = engagement

R = positive relationships

M = meaning (purpose and hope as well)

A = accomplishment

While this model serves well as a screening tool for checking whether people in general are thriving or not, I think that there are particular risk and protective factors that need to be in place to address the specific emotional needs and social and emotional development of children with SEND. By combining this model with Elliot's model and the self-assessment screening tool for adults working with the child with SEND, we stand a good chance of optimising learning and life opportunities.

Outcomes for Morale and Emotional Well-being

The maintenance of social inclusion and a range of other characteristics and behaviours can result from personal development. These may be achieved through the application of Positive Psychology. Growth factors, such as new-found enterprise, creative endeavour, etc., may be identified. The child may be helped to apply such characteristics through the use of different develop-mental pathways or using resources that may be developed. Such growth may lead to new meaning or accomplishments and therefore actively contribute to emotional well-being.

Summary

In this chapter we have:

- revisited the common concerns regarding psychological factors evident when children are faced with the adversity of a special educational need or disability, e.g. loss of identity, learned helplessness, self-worth, accept-ance of disability, motivation, etc.;
- presented the competing research findings which address the need for positive interventions to offset such difficulties;
- introduced the Positive Psychological paradigms such as learned optimism, post-traumatic growth and strengths-building as an evidence base for proactively supporting the EWB of children and young people with SEND.

4
Implications for Classroom Practice

Chapter overview

We have examined the implications of what we know about EWB in children and young people with SEND and the potential contribution of Positive Psychology. We will now consider the implications for classroom practice and offer a framework for promoting EWB at an individual, family, peer group and school level. An assessment of the protective factors that may or may not be in place is also introduced. This self-assessment tool for practitioners reading the book will help them appraise their current practice in relation to promoting the EWB of children and young people with SEND.

We will then consider how this may contribute towards the assessment of children with SEND who may be at risk of developing emotional and behavioural difficulties and low EWB. The checklist items are described in more detail in the following chapters with a view to helping the practitioner recognise risk factors in individuals and develop strategies to offset them.

As well as the self-assessment tool, this chapter also introduces the factors related to health conditions that may influence the EWB and motivation of the child as well as putting forward the case for 'systemic optimism'.

Key phrases

Deteriorating conditions; dyslexia; epilepsy; fatigue; muscular dystrophy; pain; protective factors; self-assessment tool; self-determination; systemic optimism

Assessment and Interventions to Promote EWB in CYPSEND

Professional practice dictates that assessment should inform teaching practice and that a Plan–Do–Review–Action cycle is desirable to inform any work plan, including individual education plans for CYPSEND.

There are many assessment tools that are used to examine aspects of children's mental health. Many of these are not available for front-line practitioners to use and are generally administered when a child is already perceived as having a difficulty such as low self-esteem, anxiety or depression. This book is about preventing difficulties like this from arising in the first place and therefore breaks new ground. In addition, many assessment tools that are self-report measures are inaccessible to the non-reader or to a child with limited conceptual development or communication skills. It is also important to bear in mind that with any approach to assessment, observation is key to gaining an understanding of children's emotional well-being. The child who is unable to communicate their distress verbally will often do so by exhibiting difficulties that cause concern. For example, a child who is resisting help from a new teaching assistant may become sullen in their presence or complain to their parents about them. The reality of the situation may be that the child may be having difficulty accepting that they have an additional need necessitating such support, and the manner in which that support is delivered is critical to the child being able to accept help or not. The adult who asks 'How can I help?' is far more likely to elicit a response than one who goes ahead and does everything for the child without asking or providing an explanation of their intentions. In addition, of course, children may need more support on some activities than others, so they will resent constant support where they have an opportunity to demonstrate their skills or work more informally within the group.

You will no doubt recognise the sorts of issues that can arise in working relationships as staff with the best of intentions try to help children in need of support. We will now explore factors and approaches that actively promote EWB by going through a process of considering our own practice. Those of you who take their professional development seriously will be aware that there is always room for professional and personal development. It is suggested that you now complete the self-assessment tool (see Appendix 2, p. 140), which you may find a useful personal appraisal of what you already know and do, and that it will provide ideas for addressing areas that you are less confident about. You will notice that unlike most research questionnaires, it does not have positive and negative statements. This is because the statements are intended as positive statements of guidance on how to deliver support through promoting protective factors. When you have finished reading the book, or the sections that you think you need to pay particular attention to, you may like to apply the strategies and complete the tool again to see how your score has improved.

Assessment of Protective Factors in Place for CYPSEND

The self-assessment tool (see Appendix 2: Checklist of Factors Supporting Emotional Well-being in CYPSEND) may be completed:

1 by a practitioner considering their own general practice towards CYPSEND; or
2 by considering one's work with an individual child; or
3 by observation of the child's behaviours as validated by other adults who know them well.

The stance to take is that the statements in the checklist model factors that are supportive of a child's emotional well-being when they have a SEND. You may find that by putting forward the statements, discussion about approaches currently taken will ensue. This may lead to productive changes in the child or adults working in the environment around them. You may also find it useful to refer to or encourage others to use the strategies described in later chapters.

Through completing this exercise you may highlight one or several areas that warrant action to further promote the protective factor illustrated by the statements. If this is the case, prioritise which factor you think needs addressing first. For example, you may decide that working on a child's self-advocacy skills may open doors to improvements in other areas. Alternatively, if you discover that a family is having difficulty being constructive in trying to support their child, you may want to hold a meeting with them and share those strategies on supporting parents (outlined in the chapter) that you have found useful.

It may be useful to apply your findings from the checklist to setting targets for action, stating the outcomes that you would like to see happening in the child's life or personal action plan. This action planning process is described, alongside other strategies in Part 3 of the book. Chapter 12 provides an overview of how the process can be applied.

The Checklist of Factors Supporting EWB in CYPSEND

This checklist is not a standardised instrument. It is intended as a screening or self-assessment tool to help the concerned practitioner overview the areas that are important for supporting EWB in children and young people with SEND. If intended as a checklist for an individual child, it is suggested that it is administered partly by interviewing or observing the young person so that further information can be elicited through discussion that can inform specific actions if necessary. For younger children or young people with a severe learning disability, it may also be completed as a checklist with a parent or carer, asking them to think of the child's perspective as they respond. In such a case, it acts as a useful discussion platform for enabling the changes in the child's life that may be necessary, e.g. making small steps towards greater independence.

The checklist is divided into areas covering the factors considered to be important for supporting adjustment in relation to SEND: autonomy/independence (referring to Chapters 5 and 8); competence (referring to Chapters 6 and 9); connectedness or belonging (referring to Chapters 7 and 10); optimism and the management of health issues (see pp. 39–40). Information about health is best completed from the medical information you may hold or with a parent or with the person with parental responsibility for the child, as they will have a clearer idea as to whether the child's epilepsy, for example, or ADHD or asthma is being well managed. The Observation Worksheet (see Appendix 3) may also help you with this. Of course, even if you score well on items, you may still like to read the relevant section in this book for new ideas or ways of being able to share good practice. Review your own professional development. If you scored well on the checklist of protective factors already, congratulations – share your good practice. However, if you think that there are areas you need to address, please read on, apply and repeat the assessment process following a period of action.

Optimism and Hope: Factors Supporting Systemic Optimism

Items that include reference to optimism and health are mentioned in the checklist. These are important factors supporting EWB, but do not neatly fall into the structure of this book, which is based on self-determination theory. Through research and practice, I have discovered that children value the adults around them being genuinely constructive about their SEND and prospects. As discussed in Chapter 2 (p. 17), it is important for psychological well-being that a child has a sound attributional style and that this is very dependent on those around them. The statements followed by 'optimism' in brackets test out the social environment of the child and whether they are experiencing a positive outlook through the people who support them as well as whether they themselves have an optimistic outlook. In the study I did with children and young people with visual impairments who had positive EWB (Bailey, 2011), a significant number of them had hope as one of their signature strengths, and there was strong agreement that hope was an important factor for them in adjusting to sight loss.

Physical Health Factors Supporting Adjustment

The items in this section of the checklist are related to Elliot's research (Elliot et al., 2002) and the factors that were found to be important influencing factors in adjustment to physical disability. Again, I have found support for these protective factors in my own research and practice. In particular, young people who live with the uncertainty of a deteriorating condition, such as muscular dystrophy, or an unpredictable condition, such as epilepsy, are at risk of experiencing challenges to their emotional well-being. The area has been little researched, but my own observations indicate that this has to do with impending loss and uncertainty about the future. The adults around them need to be empathic to their situation at such times and take measures to restore their sense of control in other ways. Keeping them fully informed of treatments and intentions is critical during periods of change.

Some children with SEND live with pain on a regular or constant basis and this should not be overlooked. If pain is interfering with a child's temperament or functioning, a referral to a clinical psychologist is indicated to facilitate pain management through the health service. Similarly, the child with SEND may have other medical needs, which, if overlooked, may interfere with their adjustment. For example, a child with poorly controlled asthma may be unable to join in games in the playground not because of their SEND, but because they do not have the energy to participate as a result of a lack of oxygen.

Finally, getting enough rest is included as a protective factor. Fatigue is a risk factor for mood and overall EWB and motivation. We are all sympathetic to the 'over-tiredness' that can ensue as a result of a young child's endeavours to explore the world with gusto as they apply their newly developing cognitive skills! However, as children with SEND grow, such needs can be overlooked. A teenager who is reluctant to complete homework may be exhausted from the physical exertion of a day at school. For example, a child who cannot access print fluently because of dyslexia may need to draw on other strengths and coping strategies to complete their work, all of which may require increased effort, attention or time to do so. It is not surprising then, even for the most well-motivated and stamina-driven young person, that at times they may be exhausted but not recognise it themselves. High achievers in particular need to be encouraged to take sufficient rest breaks to enable them to maintain their performance. Parents and teachers need to be on the lookout for misinterpreting tearfulness or hostility as a profound problem when all the young person needs is to be encouraged to take care of him/herself and to have sufficient rest.

Good sleep patterns are important too for concentration and general health. Again, if difficulty in getting to sleep or remaining asleep is a persistent problem, a referral to the GP is indicated so that they may consider whether the family needs help with the management of this, such as a referral to a consultant paediatrician or clinical psychologist. Some children with complex medical needs may become so physically exhausted after some activities that they will be physically sick (remember the term 'sick and tired'?). If parents and professionals are confused or concerned about the underlying cause for such symptoms, it is important to seek the advice of a paediatrician who may be able to explain why such symptoms are persistent and provide guidance in the management of routines to minimise the effects of physical fatigue.

By now, you have gained many insights into the child's perception of the way their difficulties interact with the environment. The knowledge gained should help to ensure that, step-by-step, protective factors are implemented to optimise their current and long-term EWB and motivation.

In Part 2, we will look at some of the areas covered in this chapter in more detail, and consider the assessments that may inform planning for the child.

Summary

In this chapter we have:

- proposed and described an assessment tool for screening for protective factors supporting the EWB of the child or young person with SEND;
- outlined that low scores in the areas of autonomy, belonging, competence, systemic optimism and physical factors indicate that action may be needed in one or more of these areas;
- highlighted the effectiveness of personal support as an example that may challenge a child or young person's EWB.

Part 2
Assessment

5
Independence

Chapter overview

This chapter is designed to help you appraise the degree to which a child experiences autonomy and independence in their lives generally as well as in the school situation. Dependency and control of one's environment are important factors when considering adjustment to additional learning needs or disability. A child's need for autonomy will vary according to factors such as upbringing, personality and opportunity. We all need to feel loved and wanted, and therefore have a degree of dependency, but at the same time we may wish to exert our own control over our lives. Children do this in a gradual way, acquiring greater independence as they grow and develop. The degree of independence they experience will also depend on what is achievable and safe within a given context.

Factors influencing a child's experience of autonomy are presented by considering individual (within-child), family/carer level and school system/community levels.

Key phrases

Autonomy; communicative intent; controllability; dependency; hope; locus of control; motivation; optimal adjustment; person-centred planning; positive emotions; profound and multiple learning difficulties; self-help skills; strengths; tetraplegia; transition

Point for Reflection

How do you value your independence?

Imagine you break your arm and are temporarily unable to make yourself a meal or to drive. What are the implications for you emotionally? How might it affect your relationships with others?

It would be natural to become very frustrated with not being able to do things the way you want if you are used to being independent. You may resent having to rely on others more and working around their plans. You may feel embarrassed about asking for help or even worry that you are asking too much of another person or people – after all, they seem very busy. Equally, you may relish a break from the chores and are used to having someone do those sorts of things for you anyway.

All of these reactions are perfectly normal and acceptable and will vary from person to person. Discussion about these feelings is essential in order to agree on an acceptable role for those being helped and for the helper – after all, both parties are affected.

As far as children's development is concerned, however, we need to ensure that they are given the opportunity to experience autonomy and are able to be as independent as possible when they leave school, or be able to feel at ease with their peers when they go on school trips etc. The need for autonomy will vary greatly with the child, their condition and the context.

The questionnaire below will help you appraise the child's current experience of autonomy and how desirable it is to them. The reasoning behind the questions are discussed straight afterwards. It is not a standardised assessment but is designed to prompt discussion around the key issues to independence.

You will note that a certain level of language skills is necessary to complete such questionnaires and therefore the language will need to be adapted to the developmental level of the child. For children who are unable to express themselves verbally, augmented communication methods should be used. Also, observation of the child's behaviour is important as children tend to 'act out' their emotional states. For example, if they are more reticent or more hostile with certain members of staff or subjects areas, this may be because there is a mismatch between how the child would like to be supported and the style of support that is offered. It is also possible that the child is more challenged in certain subject areas and their ability to engage with the topic is restricted, thus adding to a sense of disempowerment. Autonomy is of course dependent on a child's level of competence and the extent to which their learning style is matched to task objectives. Such issues are discussed in Chapters 6 and 9 (pp. 57 and 95).

Worksheet: My Support

Directions

Complete this questionnaire with a child or young person that you know. Use the Observation Worksheet (see Appendix 3) alongside this process to record your observations about specific issues that arise. Note that the questions serve as examples of questions you may consider. You may wish to ask alternative or additional questions that are particularly relevant to the individual child or young person. When you have completed the process, if necessary, turn to Part 3 of this book to help you to develop a plan of action to promote EWB in the child you are working with. When you have read the introduction to the questionnaire (on the following pages) and are ready, continue, following the instructions as follows:

Read out:

> The following statements are about how you cope with your special educational needs or disability [you may substitute the term for the condition that the child has and is used to using if you prefer]. Afterwards, we will

Activity 5.1

		Would you like this to be more or less? Why? Which activity? Who? How? (Notes)	Actions needed
A1 Friends and family ask whether I need help rather than assuming they know how to help.	1----------10		
A2 I like doing well to please myself rather than other people or for rewards.	1----------10		
A3 I am given the freedom to make real choices.	1----------10		
A4 I am able to take part in sport or other physical activity regularly.	1----------10		
A5 I have the opportunity to take care of myself, e.g. cooking.	1----------10		
A6 Teachers ask whether I need help rather than assuming they know how to help.	1----------10		

Emotional Well-being for Children with Special Educational Needs and Disabilities ©
Gail Bailey, 2012 (SAGE)

1ake a plan of action based on what you tell me. The idea is to help you
) get the right sort of support for you.

On a scale of 1–10 put an X where you think you are when you think of
the statement next to it. For example, if you disagree, put a cross here:

1---X---10

If you agree a lot, put a cross here:

1--X-----10

In Chapter 8 (p. 85), we will look at the strategies that can be applied to address
the need for greater autonomy, including case examples. However, here we
will now examine the factors to look out for when working with a child with
SEN that may impact on their ability to do the things mentioned in the questionnaire in Activity 5.1. We will consider these factors at child or young person, family and school or community level.

Child Level

Dependency and Control

No one would advocate leaving a child or young person with tetraplegia to
get on with their tasks totally independently unless they had the right sort of
technology or other resources in place to assist them in their endeavour and
one was sure that they were able to function optimally and were happy to
work in this way. Neither would one stand by and watch a child struggle and
fall further and further behind their peers. The idea behind these statements is
to elicit the child's perspective on the degree of autonomy they experience in
attempting to function in their daily lives.

This is important, as we saw in the last chapter, for the child's sense of control
over their situation. Some children, by personality or circumstance, will be
more dependent than others and this dependency may vary from one context
to another. This is fine if the child is happy with this, and especially if they
are making good progress and can engage in a range of activities. However,
if they are aware that they do not have the chance to make real choices, it is
worth discussing whether they would like to have a greater opportunity to do
more by themselves or to have the opportunity to have more choices. This
may mean making observations about what the child is capable of achieving,
in what context and with which learning style and aids. In the longer term,
this is not just important for EWB, but also for motivation, especially as pressure mounts for them to become as independent as possible as they approach
the transition to adulthood. I advocate the use of measures to introduce small

steps towards making choices and autonomy from an early age. It is an issue that is revisited in Chapter 11, which offers guidance for parents and other carers (see p. 122). A person-centred planning approach involving other agencies to provide professional guidance on what may or may not be appropriate for the child is important where a child has complex medical needs.

When working with individuals, I commonly come across the problem of young people resenting the type of support they receive at home or in school. By the teenage years, as they develop their new identity and struggle to secure greater independence from adults, the problem can become exaggerated and manifest itself in sullen or hostile reactions due to difficulty in communicating their feelings about the situation or in being listened to. Such a case (low scores on A1, A3, A5 and A6) indicates a need to take action with adults supporting the child to promote a greater sense of autonomy. In such a case, the box for action would be ticked and actions planned.

Communicative Intent

Some children with profound and multiple learning difficulties may struggle to make their needs known to those around them. In such cases it is paramount that adults working with them observe behaviour very closely for signs that can help the child communicate to others. For example, a child may be able to eye point in response to a query. Having this recognised could mean a breakthrough in accessing learning opportunities through just being able to exercise choice. It goes without saying that when people around a young person are responsive enough to recognise communicative intent, it will help them to achieve greater control and autonomy in their lives.

Motivation and Locus of Control

Statement A2 is about gauging whether a child is internally motivated to learn or try out new things. Again, discussion or observation quickly reveals whether they are driven by external rewards, such as treats or stickers, or withdrawal of privileges. This item is important because a sense of engagement is important to a person's potential to flourish. Young people are more likely to become engaged if they find the tasks set interesting to them. Of course engagement is also dependent on their ability to access the activities presented. The value of task analysis, so that a young person can engage as autonomously as possible, cannot be overemphasised. Such issues are also considered in the chapters on competence (Chapters 6 and 9, pp. 57 and 95).

Self-help Skills

Item A4 is included in this section as it tests whether the child is provided with opportunities for developing social skills and self-help skills outside the school situation in less structured settings. This is important for the development of self-determination and life skills as the child grows up. Of course, as well as this aspect of the statement, group physical activity is a recognised antidote to stress and offsetting low mood or depression. Such activities, if appropriate to the child, greatly enhance their range of positive emotions.

Hope Factor

Hope has been associated with the behaviour of children for over thousands of years. In spite of this, there has been little research into the topic until relatively recently. Snyder et al. (1997) devised a scale for measuring hope in children and their abstract for the research paper outlining the properties of the scale reveals some relevant issues for the children we are concerned about here:

> Assuming that children are goal-oriented, it is suggested that their thoughts are related to two components – agency and pathways. Agency thoughts reflect the perception that children can initiate and sustain action toward a desired goal; pathways thoughts reflect the children's perceived capability to produce routes to those goals. Hope reflects the combination of agentic and pathways thinking toward goals. (Snyder et al., 1997: 399)

This has great relevance to children as it is crucial for them to experience a sense of mastery over their environment and learning processes. This is closely associated with motivation and competence. It is also important that they can see a way of achieving their goals, possibly by tapping into their strengths and skills or into new developments in technology or medical research.

The questionnaire below is drawn from my research into young people's views on the significance of these factors. It was also interesting to note that in the population of children and young people with positive emotional well-being that I interviewed, a significant proportion of them experienced hope as a signature strength.

Worksheet: My Goals

Directions

Complete the checklist below with a young person that you know. Use the Observation Worksheet (see Appendix 3) alongside this process to record your observations about specific issues that arise. When you have completed the checklist, turn to Part 3 of the book to help you to develop a plan of action to promote EWB in the child you are working with.

Read out:

On a scale of 1–10, put an X where you think you are when you think of the statement next to it. For example, if you disagree, put a cross here:

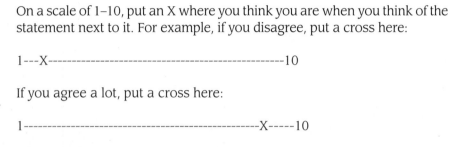

1---X--10

If you agree a lot, put a cross here:

1--X-----10

While this questionnaire is not a standardised instrument, it provides a baseline for observations about a child's hopes and aspirations – which we know from research are strongly associated with optimal adjustment in people following acquired physical disability (Elliot et al., 2002).

Low scores on this indicate a need for action planning to address this. Strategies, including the role of adults around the child, will be discussed in Chapter 8 (p. 85).

Questionnaire: My Health

As discussed in Chapters 3 and 4, physical factors have an important role to play in determining the degree of mastery a child experiences over their life. If someone is distracted by pain or fatigue, they may also struggle emotionally and become more dependent as others around them step in to assist. For this reason, an assessment related to physical factors is placed here so that one may gauge the degree to which health issues are managed optimally and to consider the possible impact on the child's sense of control over their environment.

Directions

Complete the checklist below with a young person that you know. Use the Observation Worksheet (see Appendix 3) alongside this process to record your observations about specific issues that arise. When you have completed the checklist, turn to Part 3 of the book to help you to develop a plan of action to promote EWB in the child you are working with.

Read out:

On a scale of 1–10, put an X where you think you are when you think of the statement next to it. For example, if you disagree, put a cross here:

Activity 5.2

		Would you like this to be more or less? Why? Who? How? (Notes)	Actions needed
O1 I like to look on the bright side of things.	1----------10		
O2 I like being hopeful for the future.	1----------10		
O3 Other people around me are hopeful about the future.	1----------10		
O4 I will be kept up to date with medical or technological advances.	1----------10		
O5 What is/are your short-term goal/s?			
O6 Do you know what you'd like to do when you grow up?			

Activity 5.3

		Would you like this to be more or less? Why? Who? How? (Notes)	Actions needed
H1	I experience little or no physical pain.	1----------10	
H2	I do not experience a sudden change in condition.	1----------10	
H3	My symptoms are stable.	1----------10	
H4	My other health conditions e.g. asthma or diabetes are managed well.	1----------10	
H5	I am getting enough rest.	1----------10	

Emotional Well-being for Children with Special Educational Needs and Disabilities ©
Gail Bailey, 2012 (SAGE)

```
1---X----------------------------------------------10
```

If you agree a lot, put a cross here:

```
1--------------------------------------------X-----10
```

If the child is clearly struggling with the impact of health conditions it is critical that strategies for managing the issues raised are discussed with parents and/ or other professionals. Of course, it is important to recognise that some children and young people do not like to admit that they are not getting enough rest and therefore, observations and discussion with family may help to validate their responses in this area. If this is the case, strategies such as Person-centred planning (see Chapter 9) and the management of fatigue needs to be considered (e.g. see Chapter 11).

Family Level

The family has an important role to play in fostering a child's sense of independence and control over their lives.

The questions below may help you to appraise factors supportive of EWB in the home context or with other adults working with the child, such as carers, teaching assistants, youth workers, etc. Professionals are more likely to see parents on a regular basis in the early years and therefore are in a position to work closely with them to provide an enabling environment. In my experience, most parents of children with SEN are glad to have guidance in this area. (You may wish to photocopy Chapter 11, 'A Parent's Guide', for parents to use.)

1 Are adults/carers patient and sensitive to needs of child?
2 Do adults 'see the child' and not just the SEN or disability? Do they know what the child's strengths are? (see Appendices 8 and 9, pp. 150 and 152)
3 Is the child's support 'enabling'?
4 Has the child been encouraged to be independent as appropriate from an early age?
5 Does the child have the opportunity to make real choices and have opportunities for developing life skills?
6 Are assumptions ever made about the child's functioning?

In Chapter 8 we will see how a child's independence may be enhanced from a young age (see p. 85).

School/Community Level

A child's sense of autonomy will be optimised if certain factors are in place. An assessment of a child's SEN, as part of your assessment practice, and further assessments by the SENCO and/or other professionals are a fundamental part of this process and there are many resources available to support the practitioner with this. Most children with SEN are taught in mainstream classrooms and it is important for class teachers and other professionals to work closely with SENCOs to assess need and implement Individual Education Plans where appropriate. However, in terms of a general approach to supporting autonomy, the following points for practice, which are supportive of autonomy, are offered as guidance:

Points for Reflection

- Are there any activities and skills that need to be taught to increase independence, e.g. use of technology to augment communication, the use of an online thesaurus to assist independent writing etc.?
- Does your classroom or work location enable the child to optimise their skills? Have you encouraged the child or young person to keep a strengths diary? (see Appendices 8 and 9, pp. 150 and 152). Are there opportunities for working with health professionals regarding implications of disability for functioning? If you are unable to do this directly, does the SENCO have access to this information?
- Does the child concerned need to acquire new skills, e.g. learning to touch type rather than relying on someone else to record their work for them?
- Are pastoral/care staff who are aware of a child's anxiety levels able to seek opportunities for enabling participation in leisure etc.?
- How much do you really know about what the child can and cannot do for themselves? Have you been making assumptions?
- If the child seems to lack confidence to ask for help if left to get on with work by themselves, do you know how to address this?

The above pointers will provide tips on how to access the sort of assessments that may be needed. More information about interventions to support autonomy is provided in Chapter 8 (p. 85).

Summary

In this chapter we have:

- provided the reader with resources to appraise the child's experience of independence and autonomy in their lives as well as specific assessments to gauge their awareness of their strengths and exposure to optimism and hope;
- outlined the importance of autonomy for the development of a child with SEND;
- highlighted the role of others around the child in influencing the development of independence and optimism;
- provided key points for families, carers and professionals to consider in planning effective support.

6
Competence

Chapter overview

An important part of the model espoused in this book is a child's sense of competence or ability to keep pace with their peers. This may be critical to a child's self-worth if academic success is a core component of their belief system, something that they may have acquired through upbringing or education. Assessment of factors such as strengths, problem-solving outlook, degree of assertiveness, effective multi-agency assessment and person-centred planning are discussed to plan towards the removal of barriers that may result from a SEN or disability.

Key phrases

Assertiveness; Attention Deficit Disorder (ADD); Autistic Spectrum Disorder (ASD); developmental co-ordination disorder; emotional intelligence; emotional literacy; engagement; interactive factors framework; Positive Psychology; problem-solving skills; self-advocacy; self-efficacy; self-worth; skill acquisition; stigma; strengths

The ethos of this book is in accord with the Positive Psychology mission of determining what is right about people rather than what is wrong. This is not to dismiss the important need to recognise when a child has an additional need or disability in order to make additional provision to address the impact of this for their learning and development. However, if one were to focus on just improving a child's limitations, one may be ignoring invaluable assets. To my mind, the education system has focused on meeting the needs or impairments in the child without fully capitalising on the innate resources or qualities that young people have which might help them enjoy a more fulfilled educational career and life. One must indeed consider the emotional impact of a child being expected to spend their school day immersed in programmes that they find particularly challenging compared to others without SEND. This highlights the need to make those activities as accessible, enjoyable and stimulating for the child as possible. As we saw in Chapter 3 (p. 26), regarding Seligman's (2011) findings in relation to flourishing, it is important that we consider the opportunities that the individual has for experiencing positive emotions, engagement, positive relationships, meaning and accomplishment. This chapter (and Chapter 9, p. 95) will consider how we can harness the strengths of a child with SEND and set about removing the barriers to engagement and accomplishment that may stand in the way of a child experiencing emotional well-being and their realisation of their sense of competence or capability.

The Recognition and Development of Strengths

In my experience, the children with SEND who come to see me often lack an appreciation of what their personal strengths and qualities are. One may argue that this is a sign of low self-worth. However, for the child with a disability or other difficulty, they may have become focused on what they cannot do rather on what their enduring personal qualities are and how these can help them in their life. Many teachers are adept at eliciting views about children's strengths already, incorporating these into individual education plans and target setting. For example, a child who is strong at practical problem-solving may be encouraged to choose activities or subjects that they feel engaged with and successful at. However, there are a range of enduring personal skills and qualities that may be overlooked unless time is taken to explore the less obvious sides of personality and character that may help with programme planning.

This is where Positive Psychology comes in again, and the following items are drawn from this extensive research base. These items are designed to initiate discussion about what a child's perceived strengths are and offer a valuable opportunity to bring observations of a child's strengths to their attention and to think about ways they may use them. I'll share more information about further strategies that I use in Chapter 9 (p. 95).

Problem-solving skills and self-efficacy are important protective factors supportive of EWB and motivation. However, they may be dependent on the child's tasks being sufficiently differentiated or tailored to enable them to succeed (see items C6, C7 and C8 in the 'My capabilities' worksheet in Activity 6.1).

For some children, who have limited support, it is crucial for them to be able to enlist support effectively. Sadly, I am often told by children who have been referred to me that they do not like to ask for help (see item C4 in Activity 6.1). There may be several reasons for this, but it is clear that in a child who lacks self-confidence or is shy by nature, they need to be taught ways of becoming more assertive and how to be self-advocates. This is not just an important skill to ensure that they do not fall behind in school, but is important for being able to enlist support socially and outside school. If you are able to address this aspect of a child's situation, you will be helping them greatly in their adult life as a young person with SEND as the world is very much a disabling place unless one can enlist the right sort of support without giving offence or embarrassment. Again, further details of how to implement strategies to address any actions required in this area are discussed in Chapter 9 (p. 95).

Worksheet: My Capabilities

Directions

Complete the following worksheet with a young person. Use the Observation Worksheet (see Appendix 3) alongside this process to record your observations about specific issues that arise. When you have completed the process, if necessary, turn to Chapter 9 (p. 95) to help you to develop a plan of action to promote EWB in the child you are working with.

Read out:

> The following statements are about how you cope with your special educational needs or disability [you may substitute the term for the condition that the child has and is used to using if you prefer]. Afterwards, we will make a plan of action based on what you tell me. The idea is to help you to get the right sort of support for you.
>
> On a scale of 1–10 put an X where you think you are when you think of the statement next to it. For example, if you disagree, put a cross here:
>
> 1---X---10
>
> If you agree a lot, put a cross here:
>
> 1--X-----10

Strengths Recognition and Development (C1 and C2)

Sometimes, children with SEN or disabilities are unable to recognise enduring personal qualities they may have. This may well depend on feedback from the social environment around them especially if adults around them have tended to focus on what they cannot do (even with the best of intentions). I regularly find that when I ask children what their strengths are, they are unable to respond without a lot of encouragement. Occasionally, they will provide a couple of answers centred on what they like doing, e.g. playing football or doing crafts, but they do not commonly understand or explain how these activities tap into their levels of energy or team-working skills or creativity.

Activity 6.1

	Would you like this to be more or less? Why? Which activity? Who? How? (Notes)	Actions needed
C1 I know what my personal strengths are.	1----------10	
C2 I know how to use my personal strengths.	1----------10	
C3 People around me remind me of the ways I have tackled problems in the past.	1----------10	
C4 I am confident enough to ask for help when I need it.	1----------10	
C5 I think that I can achieve things that I set out to do.	1----------10	
C6 I have referrals, assessments and reviews which provide actions for my personal plan.	1----------10	
C7 I am learning new skills to replace the old ones, e.g. touch typing/Braille.	1----------10	
C8 I have my additional needs met effectively.	1----------10	

It may be argued that most young people have difficulty in knowing what their strengths are. However, it is even more important for adults working with children with SEND to know how to help them recognise their strengths in order to maximise these in overcoming the adversity that their restrictions present. This is also important for building self-worth and helping to plan activities that gives them meaning and purpose.

There is another important reason for paying attention to this and that is to help the young person combat stigma around their disability and to remind them that they are 'Rosie, the girl who can play the clarinet and has a cracking sense of humour' rather than 'Rosie, the girl who is unable to read at the level expected of her age'. This approach reinforces the celebration of diversity in a positive way by encouraging others around the child to see Rosie as a person and not just as a person with a disability.

Point for Practice

Here is a top tip for adjusting to any disability:

Accept what you struggle with or cannot do. Focus on the things you CAN do. Parents and other adults around the child have an important role in modelling acceptance of limitations in a constructive way.

Personal Strengths (C1)

If a child has difficulty in recognising their strengths, it may be useful to assess them or to use a card game described below which is based on the internationally recognised strengths assessment tool used in the Children's Strengths Survey (Seligman, 2003):

Make a set of cards with a strength written on one side and examples of how one might use the strength on the other. Here are some examples (adapted from Seligman, 2003, with the kind permission of the author):

1 *Curiosity*

Examples:

I am interested in finding out about how things work.

I like reading or listening to stories/books as I am interested to find out what happens next.

2 *Love of learning*

Examples:

I can learn things by myself from reading/listening to books and listening or watching the TV.

I am really pleased when I understand something that was at first difficult for me to learn.

3 *Judgement*

Examples:

I can stop and think what I am going to say to my friends, to make sure it won't hurt their feelings.

I don't join in if other children/young people are being unkind to someone else.

4 *Creativity*

Examples:

I like pretending and making up games for my friends and I to play.

I like inventing things, e.g. making up songs or music, painting or making pictures or shapes with different materials.

5 *Social intelligence*

Examples:

I know the importance of being able to listen when someone else is speaking in class.

If I am working in a group, I can wait to take my turn.

6 *Perspective*

Examples:

I am proud when I have done some good work in class and I can be proud of my class mates when they have done some good work also.

Some children in my class are not always friendly to others; I don't like playing with them when they are like this.

7 *Courage*

Examples:

I can stand up for myself.

I can tell someone if I am not happy about what they are doing.

8 *Stamina*

Examples:

> If I find something hard to do, I will try again until I learn how to do it.
>
> I know that if I keep trying with something that I find difficult, it will get easier to do.

9 *Integrity*

Examples:

> I don't talk about my friends behind their backs.
>
> I can be asked to carry out a message or do a job for my teacher or by my family and I can be trusted to do it honestly.

10 *Kindness*

Examples:

> If any of my friends are sad or unhappy, I like looking after them and cheering them up.
>
> I can think about how others may be feeling before thinking about myself, and I can be helpful and kind to them.

11 *Affection*

Examples:

> I know it is important to show people that you care about them.
>
> I care about my pets, brothers, sisters and friends.

12 *Teamwork/citizenship*

Examples:

> I like helping the younger children at school, and playing with them if they don't have a friend at playtime.
>
> I enjoy helping out at our school fair/concert/sports day.

13 *Fairness*

Examples:

> If I have to pick someone to work with in a pair, I pick a different person each time from my class.
>
> If I have a new toy or game, I let my friends each have a turn.

14 *Leadership*

Examples:

> If I am the leader of a group I make sure everyone gets a turn to talk and I listen to what they are saying.

> When I am the leader of our group, I am good at thinking of different ways that we can do something.

15 *Self-control*

Example:

> I can sit still and not fidget in class.

> I can do my homework by myself without being asked, even if I am not in the mood.

16 *Wisdom*

Examples:

> If other children are messing about in class, I don't join in with them.

> If there is a fall out at playtime or break, I tell the teacher the truth about what has happened.

17 *Humility*

Examples:

> I understand and follow the class rules, and I know why we need them.

> I don't try to be the first in a queue when we are asked to line up at school; I am happy for others to go before me.

18 *Appreciation of art, music or nature*

Examples:

> I like it when we play with the percussion instruments in music.

> I like animals and learning about wildlife and nature more than most.

19 *Gratitude*

Examples:

> When someone helps me to do something I find hard, I try to find a way to help them too.

> I always say thank you if someone helps me, or if they give something to me.

20 Hope

Examples:

I often think that things will get better in the future.

I look on the bright side of life.

21 Spirituality

Examples:

I understand that if you say something unkind to someone it may hurt their feelings.

My friends and I all like different footballers/games/TV programmes/religions. I know that this is OK, as we can all like or find meaning in different things.

22 Forgiveness

Examples:

If my friends say something that is not nice to me, and later they say are sorry, I try to forgive them.

If I say something unkind, or do something that is wrong, I know that this is not alright and I say sorry to the person, or I own up to what I have done wrong.

23 Humour/playfulness

Examples:

I like making up games for my friends and I like to play or tell jokes. My friends like it when I make the games up or tell jokes.

I can make my friends laugh when they are sad.

24 Zest/enthusiasm

Examples:

I love to feel excited about things I am going to be doing in the school holidays and at weekends with my family.

I look forward to going to school each day and playing games with my friends.

*25 Problem-solving

Examples:

I like to solve puzzles, e.g. jigsaws or word puzzles.

If something is difficult, I like to set about trying to find a way around it.

Grown-ups tell me I am good at solving problems.

*26 *Assertiveness*

Examples:

I know how to ask for help when I need it.

I think my needs are just as important as anyone else's.

I have added two extra items to the list (marked with asterisks) as two qualities that are important in helping a child to adjust to a disability: problem-solving ability and assertiveness.

The strengths assessment that I use in my research and practice at the moment is the Children's Strengths Survey (Dahlsgaard, in Seligman, 2003). This was adapted in the USA from the Values in Action Inventory for Adults (Peterson and Seligman, 2004). It takes about 20 minutes to administer and can be read out if the child prefers. It usually identifies four or five signature strengths for the child and encourages a lot of rich insight into the child's life and interests. I use it with children up to the age of 15, as long as they can understand the language content, although I tend to replace some of the language. For example, I replace 'citizenship' with 'team working' since the items seem to tap into the child's ability to work as part of a group.

For young people with reading ages of 16 or above, the Realise2, which was recently developed at the Centre for Applied Positive Psychology in the UK (see www.cappeu.com) is available. This is particularly useful for periods of transition as it is based on the energy, performance and usage of realised strengths as well as unrealised strengths. It offers a useful model for encouraging personal development and planning growth towards goals.

For younger children, you can play games as a group, asking children to 'strengths-spot' with their friends.

Problem-solving (C3)

This quality tends to be an enduring characteristic as long as a person is given opportunities to develop it. It is another reason for providing an environment where a child or young person is given choice and control through effective, enabling support (see Chapter 8, p. 85). In the research I did with young people with visual impairments (Bailey, 2011), they thought that adults reminding them of past problems they had solved was important. Certainly, in casework I have found it empowering to young children to have their attention drawn to some aspect of cognitive problem-solving that they have completed successfully. Relating such capabilities to other areas in which they struggle can be productive. It is important to nuture problem-solving skills because they help the child to become more autonomous as they develop a greater sense of control. They may positively influence motivation and academic success too. They also help to build hope and confidence.

Assertiveness (C4)

Another personal quality that comes in useful if you have a SEN or disability is assertiveness. At times, the young person may need to enlist the support of others in order to get started with a task, and unless they can make their needs known this can be a problem. Research shows that people who are extrovert in personality are better at enlisting support when needed (Elliot et al., 2002). It goes without saying that being able to stand up for oneself is also an important factor in maintaining and developing competence and life-skills. This taps into social and emotional development and the development of self-advocacy.

For some children, assertiveness and self-advocacy is not a problem (especially if they are extrovert in nature). However, if adults have noticed that a child is reticent in seeking help in the classroom, or is experiencing problems with being bullied or is not responding appropriately to children's curiosity about their condition, proactive intervention may be necessary. In Chapter 9 (p. 102) we will look at strategies to promote assertive approaches to bullying and self-advocacy through script-writing. The latter strategy is particularly helpful where a child is shy by nature or has a communication problem that makes on-the-spot responses difficult.

Self-efficacy (C5) and Skill Acquisition (C7 and C8)

According to Albert Bandura (1977), self-efficacy is the individual's belief in their capacity to apply the cognitive, motivational and behavioural resources needed to perform in a given situation. Item C5 is included in the worksheet to gain insight into the child's ability to experience this important adaptive and performance factor. Of course, whether the child experiences it or not will undoubtedly depend on the extent to which their educational needs are met and whether they are able to participate in other activities comfortably. A low score here indicates a need to consider whether they are able to engage comfortably with work set for them. It is important to probe further as the child may feel more able to cope in some activities than others, which in turn indicates a need to review provision in areas where a child seems to have low capacity for task completion.

Items C7 and C8 are included to check whether there are new skills that need to be learned. Such skills may help with the degree of mastery that a child may feel over their activities (C7). For example, after years of printing their work out slowly (rather than using joined-up handwriting), a student with developmental co-ordination disorder may leap at the opportunity to learn to touch type on the recommendation of an occupational therapist or following an ICT assessment. The other factor that participants who took part in my research thought important was having their needs met effectively (C8). An example of this would be a supply teacher knowing how to audio-describe written instructions from demonstration software, thereby removing any barriers preventing access for the child with a visual impairment. It is good practice for heads of department to pass on crucial information about barriers for children with SEND to cover or supply staff.

Effective Person-centred Planning (C6)

In my day-to-day practice as an educational psychologist, I find that an interactive factors framework (see Frederickson and Cline, 2009) is a useful way of considering how cognition, biological factors, behavioural factors, environmental and management factors influence a child's development. It is a good way of ensuring that a child is enjoying engagement and mastery in their learning environment. Of course, a Plan–Do–Check–Review–Act approach to the child's learning programme is still important and should be built on a good baseline assessment. The best Individual Education Plans (IEPs) that I have come across have specific and measurable targets that actively involve the child and parents in the target-setting and review process.

The continuous and effective involvement of young people and their families in planning and decision-making is important so that people are properly empowered and enabled to influence choices and outcomes. Approaches that facilitate this, such as person-centred planning, are becoming more widespread but effective partnership involving joined-up working with all agencies must be the central principle. The approach advocated in this book is supportive of the child's capacity to have their voice heard in the process by providing strategies to enable themselves to self-advocate (see Chapter 9, p. 105).

Effective Person-centred Planning to Address EWB (C6)

As well as considering the educational needs and competencies of the child, there is a need to consider the sets of emotional competencies that a child has. 'Emotional literacy' is the term widely used in the UK to describe the acquisition of emotion-relevant knowledge. Most emotional literacy programmes target the teaching of competencies considered important to children's emotional and social development. Typically, they target the perception of emotions (e.g. the ability to recognise emotions through facial expressions) and the management of emotions (e.g. anger management).

It is critical to recognise that children with SEND require modifications to such programmes if they are to be able to access and fully participate. The four branches of the Salovey and Sluyter (1997) model of emotional intelligence are helpful as a framework for understanding the impact of a child's SEND for emotional competency. Their model is considered to be robust, and social and emotional literacy programmes are often based on this theory. For example, there are many resources for younger children based on the perception of emotions through the recognition of facial expressions. Table 6.1 provides three examples of conditions and possible barriers that may impact on children being able to access emotional literacy programmes.

It is necessary, then, to have a good understanding of the child's SEN or disability to appreciate whether there are likely to be any implications for their social and emotional development and ability to access the personal, social and health education resources widely available. By working closely with the PSHE professionals in schools, special needs co-ordinators (SENCOs) are key practitioners in addressing such issues. If there are any doubts about the

Table 6.1 Examples of barriers to emotional literacy programmes

SEND	Barriers to perception of emotions	Barriers for perceptions facilitating thought	Barriers to understanding emotions	Barriers to managing emotions
ADHD	Child may have a delay due to inattentiveness	Impulsivity may override the links to be made between perceptions and consequences	There may be gaps in acquiring age-appropriate language skills, empathy or social understanding	Overactivity, impulsivity and inattentiveness may hinder their ability to regulate their emotions
Visual impairment	If child has had no vision from infancy, they will not be able to access facial expressions unless they have had other forms of feedback from others	Unless other pathways have been found to facilitate thought and language around perceptions of emotion, they may have a gap in emotional understanding and vocabulary	They may have a limited feelings vocabulary and delayed social cognition	They may become isolated and lack social understanding and skills
ASD	Difficulties in language and social cognition impair perception of emotion in self and others	A lack of shared understanding will inhibit the child's ability to develop empathy and develop a feelings vocabulary	The lack of understanding of their emotions and of the social world can lead to a visceral expression of emotions, such as severe anxiety presenting as challenging behaviour	Emotional dys-regulation is apparent until such a time as mutual regulation leading on to self-regulation is achieved

implications of a child's SEND for their social and emotional development, it is advisable to meet with the educational psychologist or the key worker with the most insight into the child's day-to-day functioning.

In Chapters 9 and 10 (pp. 95 and 111), we will examine case studies of children with the SENDs detailed in Table 6.1 to see how we might select strategies to help with the removal of these barriers to social and emotional competence. In these chapters, we will also look at proactive strategies to offset risk factors to emotional well-being of children with SEND.

Summary

In this chapter we have:

- seen how important it is to elicit the child's view of their capabilities and how well they feel their SEN is being met since this acts as a pointer towards the need to review their educational programme planning;
- examined how the identification of children's strengths is a key part of the process of enhancing capability;
- shown how the removal of the potential barriers to emotional competency are important elements of assessment.

7
Connectedness

Chapter overview

A major risk factor in the lead up to or following a diagnosis or identification of additional needs is a sense of isolation or losing one's place. Therefore, in this chapter we will consider the child and family's response to their SEND as this adjustment phase is pivotal to maintaining social connections. We will consider emotional support for the child as well as the instrumental support necessary for promoting and sustaining belonging or inclusion.

We will also look at the relatedness component of Ryan and Deci's (2000) self-determination model and how it relates to children with SEND. For many years I have used the term 'connectedness' because it underlines the need to join connections in an instrumental way. I find it useful to illustrate the main objective of inclusion, as I see it: to help a child to find their place and a sense of belonging to their community. This chapter builds upon the factors covered in Chapter 5 on independence and Chapter 6 on competence in that a child has to have a well-developed sense of who they are and of their capabilities in order to apply them to a social context.

Following on from this, we will consider the child's social status and whether or not we need to intervene to provide instrumental or emotional support to strengthen connections.

Key phrases

Acceptance of disability; adjustment phase; belonging; Disability Discrimination Act 2005; emotional responses; feedback; grief reaction; loss; multi-agency working; pastoral support; psycho-social effects; social and emotional development; social communication; social exclusion; social skills; sociograms

The Emotional Response

Individual Level

How do we know if a child has emotional needs in response to their SEND? The answer to this is observation. A child who has previously been outgoing may become sullen or withdrawn, or their motivation and performance may be affected. At home they may change their sleep or feeding habits or may become more withdrawn or moody. Ensuring that their needs are being met will help maintain self-confidence and participation, as mentioned in previous chapters. Experience has taught me that sometimes when a child is referred to me for emotional problems, there is a need to review how their academic and social needs are being met rather than analysing their home situation, although this can be a common difficulty too. This is largely because needs change and can become an issue as a child develops, e.g. a decline in one or more of the senses or an increased demand on a child's ability to reason. Sometimes practitioners find that children will express themselves in terms such as 'why me?' This is a sign that the child has yet to accept their needs or disability, or is going through a period of questioning it again if there has been a complication or deterioration. Such disclosures need to be acknowledged and taken seriously. At the very least it is important to let the child know that it is natural to have such feelings when one faces a challenge, but that with the right sort of help or support over time, people come to terms with their difficulties and adapt successfully. Normalising the situation and linking it to other people reduces the feelings of isolation the young person is experiencing.

Additionally, by taking this approach you are taking blame away from the child, which is important if they have a medical condition outside their control. Unless you feel confident about having the time and experience to provide further emotional support, it is advisable to ask the child whether they would like to speak to someone about these feelings again. Also check who they can go to for a pep-talk if they are having an off-day. Most children have an adult they can trust and rely on for a degree of pastoral support. Make sure that this person knows that the child has expressed these views (of course, asking the child's permission to do this).

Point for Reflection

Who would you refer a child to if they said this to you and wanted to talk to someone about this further?

As well as the pastoral support available to the child normally, you may have access to school counsellors, educational psychologists or youth workers who can help to support a child through an adjustment phase. If they claim not to know much about the child's SEND, set up a meeting with the SENCO or educational psychologist so that they may share the background and knowledge of the child's needs and strengths, and help to develop solutions to the implications of the needs.

Further strategies to develop a child's resilience are discussed in Chapter 10 (p. 111).

Family Level

In order for a child to receive positive and responsive support with their difficulties at home they need parents who are emotionally available to them. Sadly, I commonly work with parents of a range of vulnerable children whose circumstances conspire against them being able to do this. Domestic violence, drug and alcohol abuse, and poverty all take their toll on a person's ability to be there for their children. Whenever we come across this situation, we do our best to provide support or direct parents to the support that may be available to them in the community.

Children with SEND may have parents who require this sort of support. However, some parents of children with SEND have additional emotional needs in response to a diagnosis (or lack of it). Parents often feel tremendous guilt about their child's difficulty, expressing the wish that it had happened to themselves rather than their child. Another response is that of searching relentlessly for a cure, or expressing anger towards professionals when the system does not have a swift solution. Such displaced emotions are signs of an emotional response often likened to a loss or grief reaction. Providing emotional support and advice through the grief process and helping to develop coping strategies during the adjustment phase are important. It is also important to provide support in overcoming ambivalence about the future to avoid these emotions leading to anxiety and depression. Timely empathy and support for parents around a diagnosis of a special need can pay dividends in terms of the parent being able to support the child through the process. See Chapters 10 and 11 for further strategies (pp. 111 and 122).

Probably the single most important piece of guidance that I give to parents who are struggling to come to terms with their child's difficulty, or who want to know what they can do to help, is for them to accept the child for who they are. Children need parental approval. Cameron and Maginn (2009) summarise acceptance and rejection behaviours (see Table 7.1). It is important to recognise that the observations outlined in Table 7.1 apply to anyone *in loco parentis*. Another acceptance behaviour that I would add is recognising and developing a child's strengths.

Table 7.1 Some examples of parental acceptance and rejection (Cameron and Maginn, 2009: 12)

Parental acceptance behaviour	Parental rejection behaviour
Celebrating a child's achievements	Ridiculing a child's achievements
Showing affection	Showing dislike
Pointing up a child's progress and developmental milestones	Comparing a child's progress unfavourably with a sibling or peer
Spending special time with a child	Too busy to spend time with a child
Sharing a mutually enjoyable activity	Imposing an activity on a child

School/Community Level

In the first chapter of the book, I highlighted the role of leisure opportunities in helping to protect people against mental health problems. In the UK, current guidelines to GPs published by the National Institute of Clinical Evidence

(NICE) recommend access to group physical activity as a preferential treatment to medication for depression. Therefore, it may be argued that the physical education curriculum is an essential part of a child's curriculum if they have SEND. It is also commonly recognised as a means for managing stress.

In addition, practitioners need to consider the role of appropriate social skills in being able to facilitate access to leisure services across the lifespan. If members of the team around the child are prioritising academic progress, they may need to be made more aware of this.

As well as awareness-raising about how to make the provision of sports and leisure for children with SEND inclusive in school, there is a need to do this at the community level. Recent consultations about the needs of adults with Autism Spectrum Disorder (ASD) in the UK (e.g. Department of Health, 2009) has highlighted this problem. It may be argued that knowledge shared through effective assessment and provision at school could help to facilitate the transition to adult services and links to service providers and transport outside school.

When completing the assessment of and observations about the child's opportunities to take part in extra-curricular activities (see below), you may elicit the psycho-social effects of a child being unable to participate without embarrassment. They may raise certain situations that have put them off attending an activity in the past. If this is the case, there may be a need to work with the family, social care or youth service providers to find solutions or to identify training needs in the wider community. Otherwise all the effort put in to provide the young person with skills while at school may be lost when they leave school. I have met parents of young people who have left school who commonly report a 'cliff edge' when a child leaves school. This needs to change. The Disability Discrimination Act 2005 strengthens people's entitlements to access to services, but there is a long way to go in terms of training and awareness-raising in the community. In Chapter 10 we will consider strategies to offset particular barriers to social skills that may arise as a result of a SEND. In particular, the impact of a difficulty with social communication for a young child with ASD is described (see p.115).

Promoting and Maintaining Connectedness

Prior to promoting strategies to enable social inclusion, it is necessary to appraise the child's situation. Assessing a child's connectedness is important for planning towards effective relationships as a first step.

In the following questionnaire (Activity 7.1), protective factors relating to people with disabilities, which have been drawn from my research and the literature, are included. You will note that some of the items (e.g. B3) are about having opportunities to socialise. Social isolation is a common concern among people with disabilities and is a risk factor for long-term social exclusion and mental health problems, as we have seen. If I had to choose one thing that I could do as an educational psychologist in trying to help a child, it would be to encourage adults working with a child to ensure that the child has at least one trusted friend either in or out of school. Some of the children I see are isolated, lonely or friendless – not a good state of affairs. (Remember that I tend to see children who are having difficulties and that many children and young people with SEND enjoy positive social relationships.) Having one trusted friend is a protective factor at many levels – not least in terms of social support and fun, but also at the level of developing self-worth and social skills through feedback.

The potential of a child to engage socially is pretty much determined by early experiences with caregivers and the availability of opportunities. As children with SEND spend more time with their families than children who are more independent, it is crucial that the support they feel around them is positive and responsive, and especially that they are included as a family member. Actions to address concerns raised in this section are discussed in more detail in Chapter 10 (p.111).

Worksheet: Towards Belonging

Directions

Complete the following checklist with a child or young person or a person who knows them well. Use the Observation Worksheet (see Appendix 3) alongside this process to record your observations about specific issues that arise. When you have completed the checklist, turn to Part 3 of the book to help you to develop a plan of action to promote EWB in the child you are working with.

Read out:

On a scale of 1–10 put an X where you think you are when you think of the statement next to it. For example, if you disagree, put a cross here:

1---X---10

If you agree a lot, put a cross here:

1---X-----10

Activity 7.1

		Would you like this to be more or less? Why? Who? How? (Notes)	Actions needed
B1 My family provides me with positive support, e.g. being patient and sensitive to my needs.	1———10		
B2 My family spends time with me.	1———10		
B3 I have opportunities to socialise outside school/ college.	1———10		
B4 I have feedback from friends or family, e.g. about my appearance or manners.	1———10		
B5 Friends and family know about the implications of my additional needs, e.g. they know when and how to help.	1———10		
B6 Teachers know about the implications of my additional needs, e.g. they know when and how to help.	1———10		

Emotional Well-being for Children with Special Educational Needs and Disabilities © Gail Bailey, 2012 (SAGE)

Positive Social Support (B1)

When I am conducting casework with children and young people, I often ask them if they have 3 wishes that could help their situation. One of the most common responses is reference to the right sort of support, and with further probing it becomes clear that adults who are patient and encouraging in their approach are more welcome than those who are hasty and critical. It is important to recognise this if one is to enable a young learner and to promote their self-worth. The other observation I have made over the years is that the emotional adjustment of children with disabilities is optimised when family are accepting of the disability and have an optimistic outlook for the future. This observation is supported by the research on acceptance of disability mentioned earlier in the book. This question is designed to elicit the child's views on the quality of the support they receive and to guide the practitioner towards appropriate action if necessary.

Quality Time (B2)

This question aims to check whether the child has a need for more attention. In our busy lives one needs to remember that time spent together is important for promoting that all important attachment factor. Carers who are too busy may give the impression to their children that they are unimportant. Again, when I come across family disharmony in casework and I ask young people what would help, they commonly reply that they would like to spend more time with one or other parent. For children who have restrictions in being able to socialise independently the quality time that they spend with their family is even more important and therefore if there is an obvious gap, it needs to be addressed. Another important thing to mention here is that adults who are stressed themselves have a tendency to transmit that stress to their children. The need to recognise this and act on it can make a huge difference to the emotional well-being of the family as a whole.

Opportunities for Socialising (B3)

This question is designed to determine the extent to which the child has opportunities for socialising in structured and unstructured settings. This is important as the young person needs to practise their social and emotional literacy in less formal situations. Also socialising is important to provide positive emotions and opportunities for sharing childhood concerns or worries and learning from others. If there are barriers to the young person being able to socialise, one may wish to explore opportunities for overcoming them.

Feedback (B4)

This question is designed to gauge whether the young person has opportunities to exchange ideas or get feedback about issues that may be important to them such as the way they look and to help them gain other people's perspectives, another facet of emotional development that is important for a sense of belonging.

Informed Help (B5 and B6)

Again, through casework I currently have young people explaining their frustration at adults who make assumptions about their learning difficulty or disability. Over the years I have found this the most important factor to consider when considering the effectiveness of a child's support. Children will sometimes refuse to co-operate with support as they do not know how to explain their difficulty with insensitive or overly helpful support. In my opinion, children should always be involved in deciding the type of help they need and in which type of activity or subject. They also need to learn self-advocacy skills in order to help explain the implications of their needs for others.

The reason that I have included these questions in this section is that if a child rejects help that has been arranged for them, they are at risk of educational failure and longer-term social exclusion.

The responses to the above questions can help to determine strategies to put in place to promote their sense of belonging as outlined in Chapter 10.

We will look at strategies to address low scores in these areas in Chapter 10, but now we will also consider how to assess a child's social status in order to determine whether they are isolated, withdrawn or friendless.

Social Status

This is an area in which school practitioners have immense experience and intuition in being able to help the child with SEND. Observations by an experienced and objective member of staff can help greatly in understanding the nature of a child's social difficulty. However, there are some useful tools that can be used to provide greater insight into the child's status within the peer group and to help plan appropriate interventions. It is common for teachers and parents to have concerns about a child's social development, but it is important to decide when to intervene or not. Many children, especially when they first start school or when they change schools, take time to settle in and it is best for friendships to grow naturally. As a rule, then, it is best to allow for a settling in period before intervening unless the child is obviously isolated and actively seeks help.

As well as observations by teacher and discussions with family members about how the child gets on socially at home, it can be helpful to use socio-grams to gain an objective appraisal of how well a child is connected within the group.

Such techniques have been in use for many years, but there are readily avail-able assessment tools on the Children's Relationships, Emotions and Social Skills (CRESS) research site at the University of Sussex (www.sussex.ac.uk/Users/robinb/). Dr Robin Banerjee at Sussex University, and colleagues at Brighton and Hove Educational Psychology service, developed a research-based social and emotional intervention called the Children's Social Behav-iour project (Banerjee et al., 2004), which will be mentioned in more detail in Chapter 10 (p.117).

Assessments Specific to Social and Emotional Development and Social Communication Skills

In order to be proactive about supporting a child's social inclusion, it is important to be aware of their social and emotional development as well as their communication development. Assessment policies vary but there is increasing recognition that front-line practitioners have a major contribution to make to the early identification and intervention for children with com-munication needs. Assessments such as WellComm (GL Assessments) are available to help practitioners intervene with children as young as 6 months to 6 years.

Where necessary, specialists such as speech and language therapists should be consulted and their advice built into the child's programme. It is impor-tant to assess these skills as a delay in expressive, receptive or pragmatic language skills may interfere with a child's ability to engage with play activi-ties at an appropriate level for their age. Expressive delay may impede their ability to make their needs known through asking questions. Receptive lan-guage delay may mean that they have difficulty following instructions, such as the use of prepositions (e.g. 'Put the doll in the playhouse'). Pragmatic language skills may mean that the child has difficulty with rules such as turn-taking. Difficulties in any of these areas can affect the child's ability to develop socially and can also lead to isolation.

In terms of general delay in development, the school nurse or community pae-diatrician will sometimes be involved with a child and will be able to provide information about social and emotional development and what barriers may prevent a child from developing play and social skills. For example, a child who has delayed motor skills will not be able to join in all play at an appropriate level. Some children will find their own creative solutions, e.g. crawling under hurdles rather than trying to leap over them. Again, the advice of medical professionals such as physiotherapists and occupational therapists should be built into the child's programme to minimise the impact on their social and general development.

If there appears to be a delay in social and emotional development, it is also advisable to check with the SENCO to see whether the involvement of an educational psychologist should be requested as most assessments in this area are only registered to specialists or educational or clinical psychologists. The educational psychologist (EP) will be interested in your observations and will sometimes give you checklists to gain further objective information about the child's social skills and other contributing factors. They may also give you checklists to provide to parents as behavioural observations in two or more settings are often required.

Sometimes, especially where a child has significant difficulty conforming to classroom rules and routines and being at ease in group situations, there may be further assessments of social communication skills, undertaken by both speech and language therapists and psychologists. Sometimes their assessments lead to further developmental assessments to explore other developmental disorders, such as autism, Asperger's Syndrome, dyspraxia or ADHD or a number of other possible difficulties. In the early years it can be difficult to make a differential diagnosis of these conditions and multi-disciplinary assessment is the preferable way forward. Again, the implications of the child's needs for social functioning will need to be taken into account in their individual programme to promote a sense of belonging. Children with autism lack social awareness and find the social world a perplexing place, but this does not mean that they do not want to belong. Some appear to be happiest with their own company and calm down when they are able to access quiet and familiar surroundings. However, as they get older, they may become more aware of their need to cope in group situations and the need for adults and peers around them to understand their behaviour. We will look at a case study related to this type of situation in the next chapter.

Sensory impairments can also have an impact on a child's communication and social development, and it is advisable to involve the specialist teachers for hearing impairments or visual impairments to gain a clear understanding of the child's functional hearing or vision for their social skills. The educational psychologist can also help with this but in some cases the child will not have been assessed by an EP.

Summary

In this chapter we have:

- examined how children with SEND often adapt successfully to a diagnosis or SEN. However, some need emotional support with this, especially at transition points. At such time, their social inclusion may be affected and it is important to help them with this.
- emphasised how secure attachment and parental acceptance of a child for who they are are central to a child's sense of self-acceptance and self-worth. Issues arising from their absence need to be addressed as early as possible;
- discussed that, in addition to potential emotional barriers to their sense of belonging, children with SEND sometimes have needs that directly impact on their ability to socialise. For example, delayed or disordered communication skills need to be addressed as early as possible to offset the potential barriers to play and social development;
- highlighted that further assessments by outside specialists are indicated if the child is isolated or if the implications of their condition for their social development is uncertain. Effective multi-agency assessment and partnership is important in optimising the child's programme to address their social development.

Part 3
A Plan of Action

8
Promoting Independence

Chapter overview

In this chapter we will examine strategies that may be used to tackle the issues highlighted by our assessment of a child's independence and autonomy, as outlined in Chapter 5.

At an individual child level, we discuss the provision of support to address a child's SEN and offer strategies to address the specific emotional needs that may arise. Case studies are provided to illustrate the application of these strategies.

The development of strengths is also examined as this is particularly relevant to a child's sense of who they are. Optimising a child's strengths is fundamental in supporting EWB in other areas, such as influencing motivation and goal-setting as well as developing competencies and a sense of belonging.

At a family and/or carer level, strategies to promote awareness-raising to encourage independence are discussed and the importance of positive social support is highlighted.

At school, community and peer-group level, the importance of removing barriers to participation is discussed, with reference to the modifications that can be made to allow a young person with SEND to flourish.

Key phrases

Asperger's Syndrome; Down's Syndrome; cerebral palsy; engagement; fatigue; hearing loss; hope theory; mobility; motivation; multi-sensory teaching; organisational skills; personal management; self-determination; self-efficacy; self-help skills; visual timetables

Effective support for a child is instrumental or practical and affective (and emotionally supportive). Practitioners are often very skilled and experienced at understanding how to promote the skills and abilities of a child, but are less confident about supporting a child emotionally. Adults working around a young person need to be aware that positive social support is important to adjust well. Patient, sensitive support that also takes into account the need for independence is a good place to start.

Self-efficacy, or the feeling that one has control over one's environment and motivation, can be encouraged by promoting real choices. Children quickly acquire roles, values, ways of behaving and ways of coping with their world within their family culture and within the context of the wider social culture. As children get older, the school culture and peer group have an increasing impact on personal outcomes.

My Support: A Child-centred Approach

Dependency and Control (A1, A3, A5 and A6)

A good parenting or caring relationship involves a subtle responsiveness to one's child, where one intervenes when the child makes a sign of some kind. In the early years, we can encourage or model 'scaffolding', mediating approaches. It may be necessary to make explicit other pathways to building the usual skills, e.g. using visual timetables where a child has a poor grasp of receptive language. Unfortunately, where children have difficulties in responding in the usual way, carers can sometimes take over control of the child's situation instead of finding alternative means of allowing them a say in their situation.

Case Study: Chesne

Chesne (5) has just started reception class. He has Down's Syndrome and has general learning difficulties which make it difficult for him to understand what is required of him in the day-to-day routines of the classroom. His teacher and assistant have noticed how passive he is compared to the other children. He also gives up easily on simple tasks devised for him and is totally dependent on his assistant.

The SENCO, Jane, checked the assessments by the paediatrician and educational psychologist and noticed that he has a strength in visual memory. Discussion with his parents revealed that they have a large family and they found that it was quicker to do everything for their son than to try to find ways of improving his self-help skills.

A visual timetable of symbols representing the activities undertaken in daily routines was introduced and Chesne was encouraged to use this to make choices during activity time as well as to guess what was going to happen next in a simple routine. In this way, he became more alert to what was required of him and more able to express his needs as well. The system was introduced at home too and over time the family noticed how smiley and interactive he had become as he was able to communicate more effectively with them all.

Over-attentiveness may lead to poor motivation as the child does not learn to handle disappointment. It may also lead to anxiety if a child does not learn how to overcome concerns about whether they can do something or not. Therefore, over-zealous parenting/caring has its downside and needs to be diplomatically addressed!

It is difficult to watch someone you love struggle with the acquisition of new skills, especially as this can involve witnessing fatigue and frustration. It is also difficult to watch a young person endure anxiety or panic in facing up to the challenges presenting themselves. A parent's instinct may well be to protect young people from such strain by leaping in with direct action. Difficult as it is, a judgement needs to be made about the impact of such action on longer-term quality of life and independence. Parents need support in enabling them to take a step back in such situations. They may also need help with dealing with their feelings regarding this approach. Some front-line professionals need help with this too.

Conversely, neglectful, unresponsive support will undermine development. For example, the child may have restricted fine motor skills because they may not have been given opportunities to crayon or use cutlery.

Over-attentiveness in young people can also lead to resentment as they struggle with self-consciousness and possibly stigma attached to having a SEND.

Case Study: Cara

Cara (11) was becoming increasingly sullen in her attitude towards school. Her form tutor called her aside to ask how she was one day as her grades were slipping and staff were finding her increasingly petulant. Cara experiences fluctuating hearing loss as she has reduced hearing in one ear that is made worse when she has recurring respiratory infections. Therefore, sometimes she needs extra help in following verbal instructions and sometimes she doesn't. Her French teacher, Miss Kay, had been getting on her nerves because she was routinely offering help with every change of activity. Cara resented this as she is a teenager who is trying to 'blend-in' and doesn't see the need for making so much fuss. She values her independence. Miss Kay tended to ask Cara 'Do you need help?', to which she got a perfunctory reply 'No', regardless of whether Cara needed help that day or not.

The form tutor, realising that her colleague was only trying to be helpful, asked Cara if she would mind if she advised all Cara's subject teachers to only ask Cara whether she wanted help when she is not working and then to say 'How can I help?' Cara agreed to this and after a couple of weeks the form tutor asked how French was going. Cara was much happier now that she felt she could explain to her teacher more about her needs.

If a teacher asks a self-conscious teenager 'Do you need help?', they are likely to get mono-syllabic answers. Just by changing to an indirect questioning style, e.g. 'How can I help?', the student has to respond and with more detail. It helps open up communication and allows the child a greater sense of control in the situation. I have made such a recommendation countless times and always with positive effect. In one case, a teenage boy told me that this small adjustment had made a greater difference to his life in school than all the other strategies put together. I think this shows how important it is to resolve breakdowns in communication between adults and teenage children when they are striving for independence.

Points for Practice

You can help in the following ways:

- By observing the child closely to see what they can and cannot do.
- By being responsive, making small actions or suggestions to help the child make the next small step by themselves, and only intervening where necessary.
- If you are working with parents or carers, by giving them 'permission to take a step back' and by gently encouraging them to think of the child's long-term interests. They are not being mean by encouraging steps towards independence from an early age.
- By making sure that the tasks set are within the child's grasp (Chapters 6 and 9 are relevant here too).
- By encouraging other adults and peers working around the child to ask 'How can I help?' rather than making assumptions about the child's needs at any point in time.

By taking this approach you will be helping to optimise the child's and family's response to A1, A3, A5 and A6 in the 'My support' assessment tool described in Chapter 5 (p. 46).

Motivation (A2)

Professionals working with children should always strive to optimise the child's motivation as the effort that a child puts in will no doubt impact on their performance. However, it should be stressed that it is preferable for a child to be internally motivated to succeed rather than being driven by external rewards such as treats for good marks. In my opinion, positive reinforcement has a role where a child has lost all sense of motivation to behave well or to work. However, the reinforcement needs to focus on the effort rather than the outcome. This is particularly important for children with SEN as they may try very hard and still not succeed unless their tasks are carefully differentiated to ensure success.

For tasks to become intrinsically motivating to a child they must be relevant and engaging to them. Therefore, it can help to understand what interests the child and to relate the tasks to these areas or sets of skills if at all possible.

Martin Seligman (2011) stresses the role of engagement in supporting emotional well-being and it is easy to see why. When a person is fully occupied by a task that they can do well, they lose sense of time, becoming absorbed in the task for the purpose of completing the task or just for doing it. Examples include people who enjoy hobbies such as art or music. One can become engaged in learning a new skill, providing barriers are removed for the child. For example, a teenage boy with ADHD, who has experienced years of being criticised for his poor handwriting, may be reluctant to write essays. Provide him with an ICT assessment and touch typing lessons, and a topic of relevance to him, and there is a fighting chance of being able to improve his motivation.

Points for Practice

You can help in the following ways:

- Find out what interests the child has.
- Provide encouragement and genuine praise for effort (this helps to build self-worth too).
- Make reasonable adjustments to allow the child to access the task at a comfortable level (see also Chapters 5 and 9, pp. 45 and 95).
- Optimise the use of their interests and strengths.

Self-help Skills/Self-determination (A4)

This aspect is closely linked to dependency and control. It is included as a separate heading because it can become a big issue as a young person enters adolescence. Even non-disabled young people struggle with self-help skills when they leave home. However, they do not face the additional challenges that living with a disability presents. For example, they may not need to learn how to ask for help with reading application forms for jobs. There is a recognised need to consider the explicit introduction of a range of self-help skills in preparation for college, work or leaving home for young people with disabilities. Encouraging autonomy from a young age can reduce anxiety in learning such new skills, but educational professionals need to work closely with parents, social care providers and other agencies to ensure a smooth transition.

Person-centred planning and unified assessments will help with this process as they become more embedded in good practice. However, it must be stressed that there is little point in meeting academic targets if we overlook the need for the young person ultimately to take up their place more fully in their community. We need to offset their increased risk of social exclusion with associated mental health risks by considering strategies to address the following:

1 *Personal management and self-care*

The young person needs to know about the implications of their SEND in order to ask for the right sort of help or to make the right choices for themselves. This will encourage independence because it will facilitate success.

Case Study: Tom

Tom (16) has Asperger's Syndrome. He gets extremely agitated if required to stand in a queue and this can lead to embarrassing situations for him and others around him as he loses emotional control. He is learning to call the doctor's surgery and explain this when making an appointment. That way when he arrives for his appointment, the receptionist knows to allow him in next to see the doctor when he arrives at the surgery.

Self-advocacy strategies like this will be discussed more fully in Chapter 9 (p. 105).

---

2 *Daily living skills, organisation, orientation and mobility*

Some young people with disabilities have great difficulty with such aspects of independence. *Aides-mémoire*, such as mobile phone technology, can assist greatly with organisational skills, as can visual timetables for young people with severe communication difficulties such as Autistic Spectrum Disorders. However, if a young person has a disability, there is often a need for a care assessment to establish a young person's needs for transition to adulthood. Adaptations may need to be made to the home environment to facilitate the young person's independence. Again, these issues should be considered at reviews of progress, particularly from age 14 onwards. Where the young person's needs are unlikely to fit the criteria for social care involvement, it is important that a person-centred planning approach is adopted to facilitate a smooth transition. Forward planning involving parents and the young person in actively acquiring these skills could make the difference between a successful transition to college or not.

3 *Career education*

Specialist careers advisors are available to vulnerable young people who may need additional support to access the workplace and to find vocation opportunities or training suited to their strengths. It is important here that the young person has a good grasp of their needs and strengths. An effective person-centred approach to the assessment of their needs will facilitate this. However, knowledge of their skills, qualities and strengths need to be actively taught to help them self-advocate when they leave school.

4 *Social interaction and leisure activities*

As mentioned in the early chapters of this book, social inclusion and physical exercise are important to mental health. In order for a young person to independently access such opportunities, they may need to be explicitly taught a range of social skills and coping strategies. These will be explored more fully in Chapter 9 (see also Chapter 6).

Hope and Optimism Factors

Research into hopeful people has found that they have greater success, gain more meaning out of life, experience better health and suffer fewer symptoms of depression and anxiety (Cheavens et al., 2006). Hope theory holds that hopeful people have the following three characteristics:

1 They have desired goals that they are motivated and enthusiastic about.
2 They have pathways or effective plans to help them find a route to their goals with built-in alternatives if a certain approach fails.
3 They have agency (self-belief and confidence in their capabilities to strive for their goals). (Leach et al., 2011: 51)

In my experience, some parents may have difficulty visualising futures for their child with SEND and therefore the child will rely on trusted peers or other mentors around them to help with this. There is an undoubted value in SEN practitioners and pastoral staff supporting children with SEN in the setting of achievable goals and directing them to strategies that can assist them in the achievement of them. If these goals can enthuse them about the future through a consideration of their interests and strengths, they are more likely to sustain effort towards them too. It should be remembered that few people actually do the things that they dreamed about when they were younger, but what is important is that they see shorter-term goals as building towards the future they aim to construct for themselves.

Hope and Medical Research and Technology

In the course of my work, I find that parents frequently undertake their own research into their child's condition, sometimes to find a cure. Some perceive this as a denial response, especially if it is sustained over time. However, I see this as a positive response as it denotes hope and a problem-solving approach. If there is no 'cure' or perfect solution to managing all the implications of a SEN or disability, it is worth periodically updating oneself in research around a certain field. Even if there is no medical solution, there may be new advances in the management of the SEND or technological solutions to problems that may help. An example of this is the increasing use of cochlear implants to minimise the effects of hearing loss compared to 10 years ago.

In my experience, parents and young people find it helpful to know that there is the possibility of new solutions in the future. It is important, however, not to raise false hopes, as this can be disappointing. Periodically in the media, one hears about miracle cures for certain conditions. It is advisable to check the objective facts behind such news items as some conditions may have many variations which may not relate to the child with whom you are concerned. When in doubt, encourage the family to consult their GP for further guidance, pointing out that it is a good thing that research is going on in the area.

Where parents confide in you their disappointment about a lack of positive outcomes in such situations, remind them of the child's capabilities and of the way we are working together to overcome restrictions. The issue of emotional support for parents will be discussed further in Chapters 10 and 11.

Factors Supportive of Independence

Family/Carer Level

- Provide positive social support by being patient and sensitive to the needs of the child.
- See the person and not just the disability.
- Provide enabling support.
- Encourage independence from an early age.
- Provide real choices and opportunities for developing life skills. If concerned about health and safety, seek professional advice from mobility specialists and from health or social care professionals for an informed opinion.
- Provide opportunities for pursuing leisure and sport activities. Local authorities employ disability sport officers who can assist with information about accessible venues and opportunities that are available locally.
- Avoid making assumptions about the child's functioning, e.g. use language such as 'How can I help?'
- Model goal-setting as a family, e.g. planning a family holiday together.
- Model an optimistic outlook on life and have contingency plans if things do not work out as hoped. Challenge negative thinking – the last thing you need to do is to reinforce the self-fulfilling prophecy of a child who thinks they are incapable of success.

School/Environmental Level

- Identify activities and skills that need to be taught to increase independence, e.g. the greater use of technology or improving social competence. This is an important part of their assessment of needs and enables effective provision.
- Draw attention to the child's other competencies to help compensate for restrictions in participation. Help them to find and use alternative pathways to accomplishing a task. Even if they cannot do the whole task unaided, help them to identify what they can do.
- Make the learning environment optimal for success, e.g. if the child concerned has a hearing impairment, are you aware of the implication of their condition for accessing aural activities? A simple adjustment, such as ensuring that you present instructions on the child's best side, may help. Have you considered asking for an environmental audit? Arrange to have a chat with an advisory teacher who specialises in certain conditions. Local authorities have a statutory duty to provide specialist teachers who are qualified in the teaching of sensory impairments. Ensuring access to the curriculum with steps enabling success is vital to academic self-worth.
- Apply multi-sensory teaching approaches so that you facilitate the use of a range of learning styles in your classroom. For example, supplementing verbal instructions with visual prompts and handouts will help the children in your class who have dyslexia, hearing impairments and Autism Spectrum Disorders. Helping children to access the curriculum in this way helps them to become less dependent on your input for reinforcement. However, it is standard good practice to survey the room to ensure that all children are engaged.
- Work with health professionals regarding the implications of disability for functioning. For example, a child with cerebral palsy may be fairly autonomous with the right aids at certain times of the day, but not at others due to fatigue factors. In such a case, it would be important to seek the advice of physiotherapists or occupational therapists for an objective opinion as well as working closely with family/carers who know the child best and how their mood fluctuates with level of challenge or fatigue.
- Seek opportunities for enabling participation in leisure and sport activities to offset anxiety. Be aware that where a SEN or disability makes it difficult for a young person to work as part of a group (e.g. autism), they may encounter difficulty with team sports and suitable modifications or alternatives need to be explored.
- Avoid making assumptions about the child's functioning. Use your knowledge of the implications of the condition but be aware that independence may vary with the context. Therefore, using questions such as 'How can I help?' are important in reinforcing independence.

- Follow the other approaches suggested for families and carers above. Systemic optimism is a very important factor for supporting autonomy and emotional well-being.

Summary

In this chapter we have:

- examined the factors that are supportive of autonomy in children and young people with SEND, e.g. the promotion of control over the environment, the need for adults to offer responsive support, the importance of intrinsic motivation and opportunities to develop self-help skills, strengths, assertiveness, hope and problem-solving ability;
- recommended strategies that can be employed at the individual, family and school/community levels and provided case studies of children with Down's Syndrome, Asperger's Syndrome, ADHD and hearing impairments;
- detailed the strategies that provide instrumental (practical) as well as affective support to address the specific emotional needs that may arise as a result of a SEND.

9
Removing Barriers to Engagement and Supporting Capability

Chapter overview

In Chapter 6 we discussed the assessment of strengths in young people, and in this chapter it will be evident how important it is for a young person to recognise their enduring qualities and characteristics if they are to be able to self-advocate. Ironically, I believe that for many years in the system intended to address a child's SEN, we have been expecting children to undergo annual reviews of their progress and attend specialist careers interviews without adequate preparation. Children need to know how to express themselves and their needs in such situations, but they also need to be able to express their knowledge of their strengths and interests if we are going to deliver effective, engaging and purposeful experiences for them in the future. It may be argued that the future system, based on person-centred planning, would serve young people better by deploying their abilities rather than focusing on what they cannot do. For example, if they need to acquire organisational skills, what personal qualities can they bring to the solution for them in their environment and how can people around them support them with this?

This chapter addresses the need to tackle particular barriers to emotional literacy that may influence a child's emotional well-being if they have a SEND.

Key phrases

ADHD; assertiveness; emotional literacy; feelings vocabulary; Positive Psychological interventions; problem-solving; self-advocacy; strengths; visual impairment

Developing Strengths

Since starting my research into optimal functioning following physical disability and visual impairment in 2003, there has been a growth in scientific evidence supporting the use of Positive Psychological Interventions (PPIs). Sin and Lyubormirsky (2009) did a meta-analysis of 51 empirically tested PPIs involving 4,000 individuals and found that they can significantly increase well-being and decrease depressive symptoms. Among the interventions studied were strengths recognition and development, learned optimism, goal setting and hope therapy, which I think are particularly relevant to the needs of children with SEND.

Although I have been using strengths recognition and development in my casework increasingly over time, I think that front-line practitioners such as teachers and youth workers are well placed to use such strategies too. After all, they are in the business of bringing out the best in young people. Indeed, there is increasing support for the integration of PPIs into Youth Work (e.g. see Leach et al., 2011).

Here I will outline the approach I take when I think that a young person would benefit from being able to recognise and develop their strengths.

1 Determine whether the young person has appropriate insight into their personal qualities and strengths. If not, assess their signature strengths, as outlined in Chapter 6 (pp. 58–66).
2 Ask the young person to write down three things that went well for them in the past week (you can record these for the child if preferred). This is, in itself, another effective PPI: gratitude is one of the 24 signature strengths that Seligman reports in his book, *Authentic Happiness* (Seligman, 2003).
3 Identify the top 4–5 signature strengths identified in the assessment process.
4 Ask the young person to identify examples when they have used their strengths recently. You can refer to the three things that went well for the child in the last week and tease out how their strengths helped them with these. This process is important to ensure that the child is able to recognise their strengths and how they actively work for them.
5 Set homework using the Weekly Strengths Diary worksheet (Appendix 8). This involves asking the child to identify when they have used one or more of their strengths for each day of a week. Arrange to see them again in about a week's time to see how they got on.
6 Look at their Strengths Diary together, again, checking that they understand how they have used their strengths. Ask them if they used any of their strengths in new situations.
7 Developing strengths. Now discuss with the child how they would like to use their strengths to help them overcome any challenges they face. It is important to discuss how they may do this and which strength/s they would use to develop the new strategy. Set some modest goals for doing this over the next week using the goal-setting Strengths Diary worksheet (Appendix 9). Explain that you'll see them again in a week to see how they have got on.
8 In a week's time meet to discuss how they got on, giving genuine praise for effort and avoid judging the child if they were unable to follow through

as planned. (In such a case, give them a chance to complete the task for the following week.) Point out how they have grown as a person and reflect with them on how it felt to develop their strengths in that way.

9 Encourage the young person to continue developing their strengths and to keep a diary of when they use them. Point out that using their strengths should become easier to them as time goes on because they are part of who they are and therefore may help them to feel more energised by finding ways of applying them more often.

10 Review the development of strengths periodically, perhaps reminding them of other qualities that were not quite in their 'Top 5' that they may also like to try using in their daily lives.

Case Study: Ben

Ben (14) has ADHD and is not getting along with his peer group. They know that they can easily wind him up and get him into trouble. He has had years of people getting annoyed with him for dropping things in class and generally becoming distracted from what he is supposed to be doing.

Ben's top 5 signature strengths were:

Zest, ingenuity, humour, kindness and team work

After keeping his strengths-spotting diary for a week, he realised that he actually uses his strength in humour and team working a lot when he plays football for the local Under 16s and that he uses his ingenuity to plan strategy when playing on his games console at home. He also uses humour and kindness to help keep his younger brother occupied while mum cooks the tea.

We used these strengths to help him make small changes in school over the next week. For example, he used his ingenuity to work out how he could join more after-school clubs and help coach the younger players in their ball skills (using kindness and team working). In class, he planned to channel his energy into doodling while the teacher was talking to help him concentrate on the important stuff rather than reacting to other things going on around him. It was important to check with the teacher that he should be allowed to doodle. His classmates soon gave up trying to get him into trouble when they realised he was ignoring them. Also, he earned some respect because they did not realise that he was so good at football as he had been avoiding playing with them for ages.

This case study illustrates how children can use their strengths to make small changes that can help to restore a sense of personal control of their situation. Children with ADHD have a medical condition that is very difficult for them to control. This can easily become a significant emotional problem for them if they are rejected by their peers and adults. While this approach will not cure the underlying health problem, it can help to improve their experiences and to develop coping strategies that are likely to work for them. Of course, it goes without saying that such approaches should be planned, applied and reviewed on a regular basis as part of their Individual Education Plan as such children regularly face new sets of challenges in varying contexts. I prefer to think of these children as challenged rather than challenging. This approach can be effective in helping to offset such challenges for them.

'Better Out than In'

You may have heard psychologists or counsellors use this expression to encourage people to share their feelings. Containment of an emotional problem by having someone to go to and unload worries or concerns can indeed be very therapeutic. However, some children have problems with this as they find it difficult to express emotions. You may be aware that play therapy or art therapy is considered more appropriate for young children than 'talking therapies', and there is a developmental reason for this. In Chapter 6 we learned about the branches of emotional intelligence: perception–understanding–thought/language–management/coping strategies.

In Table 6.1 (p. 69), highlighting barriers to these abilities that may present with certain conditions, an example of ADHD was given. Ben had struggled in the areas highlighted, and as well as using his strengths to improve the situation for him, he benefitted from counselling. At first, this was problematic because he had difficulty expressing himself due to a limited feelings vocabulary. In an environment free of distraction, it was possible to expand his ability to express his feelings by introducing a wider range of words.

Many emotional literacy resources have an appendix of lists of words expressing feelings – feelings vocabularies or inventories are useful resources for the practitioner. A good way of using such lists is to draw attention when a child or group uses a feelings word – check if it is in the list and encourage them to add it to their word lists or diaries. This not only gives children permission to talk about feelings, but by drawing attention to it in context, you will be helping them to understand, label and identify whether this is something they need to do something about or not. A child who uses Braille can include their new word in their Braille dictionary. A child who has a severe communication difficulty may benefit from photographs or pictures of scenarios to augment the vocabulary being built.

I have included a simple list here for your use. It is not as comprehensive as some, but I have chosen words that are in plain English and organised them into two groups of feelings.

Feelings when your needs are not satisfied:

AFRAID

apprehensive

dread

foreboding

frightened

mistrustful

panicked

petrified

scared

suspicious

terrified

wary

worried

ANNOYED

aggravated

disgruntled

dismayed

displeased

exasperated

frustrated

impatient

irritated

ANGRY

enraged

furious

incensed

irate

livid

resentful

AVERSION

appalled

contempt

disgusted

dislike

hate

horrified

hostile

repulsed

CONFUSED

ambivalent

baffled

bewildered

dazed

hesitant

lost

perplexed

puzzled

torn

DISCONNECTED

apathetic

bored

cold

detached

distant

distracted

indifferent

numb

removed

uninterested

withdrawn

DISQUIET

agitated

alarmed

disturbed

perturbed

restless

shocked

startled

surprised

troubled

turmoil

uncomfortable

uneasy

unnerved

unsettled

upset

EMBARRASSED

ashamed

flustered

guilty

self-conscious

FATIGUE

burnt out

exhausted

lethargic

listless

sleepy

tired out

weary
worn out

PAIN

agony
anguished
bereaved
devastated
grief
heartbroken
hurt
lonely
miserable
regretful
remorseful

SAD

dejected
depressed
despair

despondent
disappointed
discouraged
disheartened
forlorn
gloomy
heavy hearted
hopeless
unhappy

TENSE

anxious
cranky
distressed
distraught
edgy
fidgety
frazzled
irritable
jittery

nervous
overwhelmed
restless
stressed out

VULNERABLE

fragile
guarded
helpless
insecure
reserved
sensitive
shaky

YEARNING

envious
jealous
longing
nostalgic
pining
wistful

Feelings when your needs are satisfied:

AFFECTIONATE

compassionate
friendly
loving
open hearted
sympathetic
tender
warm

CONFIDENT

empowered
open

proud
safe
secure

ENGAGED

absorbed
alert
curious
engrossed
fascinated
interested
intrigued
involved

spellbound
stimulated

EXCITED

amazed
animated
astonished
dazzled
eager
energetic
enthusiastic
invigorated
lively

surprised
vibrant

EXHILARATED

blissful
ecstatic
elated
enthralled
radiant
thrilled

GRATEFUL

appreciative
moved
thankful
touched

HOPEFUL

encouraged
expectant
optimistic

INSPIRED

amazed
awed
wonder

JOYFUL

amused
delighted
glad
happy
jubilant
pleased
tickled

PEACEFUL

calm
centred
clear headed
comfortable
content

equanimous
fulfilled
mellow
quiet
relaxed
relieved
satisfied
serene
still
tranquil
trusting

REFRESHED

enlivened
rejuvenated
renewed
rested
restored
revived

(This list has been adapted from the Center for Non-violent Communication website: www.cnvc.org, downloaded 23 August 2011.)

Another word I would add into the 'needs being met' list is 'energised'. Think of an activity or a day that went well in work and how energised you felt. When we are able to use our strengths and capabilities, we feel energised. This is a need to be met, isn't it?

The development of a basic feelings vocabulary is a very important competency. Even if the child does not go for counselling, they will be enabled to talk about their feelings to trusted friends or relatives. It is also an important competency as it helps the child to manage feelings in ways that are more helpful to them than boiling over with anger and frustration. Another particularly useful range of vocabulary refers to fatigue or tiredness. The child who is drained by their SEND over the course of the day may become emotionally labile. It is useful for them to communicate this to the adults around them to avoid coming over as insolent or lazy. A feeling vocabulary is also important in the building of assertiveness as a key competency and protective factor.

Problem-solving

Research has established that having a problem-solving approach can help with managing the challenges of physical disability (Elliot et al., 2002). Certainly, I have found through casework and research that children think it is an important factor.

Most children and young people are familiar with problem-solving through play and leisure activities. It can be helpful to draw attention to times when they have used these skills, e.g. to get to the next level on a strategy game on their games console. This is particularly important when they get 'stuck' with trying to resolve a personal or academic situation and it can really help to remind them of past problems they have solved to increase their sense of agency and the prospect that they can do the same again. For children faced with multiple challenges who also get fatigued from time to time, it can be really helpful to restore their sense of control in this way, all of which is very supportive of autonomy.

Problem-solving is an important attitude to adopt when 'bouncing back' or building resilience. We will look at a relevant approach to building the latter when we look at strategies to promote competency.

Assertiveness

Being able to stand up for yourself and to see yourself as of equal value to others is important to a sense of autonomy. There are plenty of resources available to practitioners about how to develop assertiveness (e.g. Rae, 2000, which is aimed at secondary school-aged pupils). When choosing resources, check that the objectives of the resources match your objectives and are accessible or modifiable for the child concerned.

In order to build assertiveness, it is useful to think of human rights.

Point for Reflection

Which rights do you think are particularly important for children with SEND?

- The right to be treated with respect
- The right to make mistakes and be responsible for them
- The right to refuse requests without feeling guilty or selfish
- The right to ask for what you want
- The right to be listened to and taken seriously
- The right to say I don't understand
- The right to ask for information

You may have observed how important it is to have self-respect in order to feel assertive. Note that each of us tends to have one of three different response styles:

- Passive – to behave as if other people's rights are more important than yours.
- Aggressive – to behave as though your rights matter more than other people's rights.
- Assertive – to behave as though you respect yourself and others equally.

A school ethos which promotes diversity and has active anti-bullying policies will be supportive of the assertive response style as well as actively encouraging recognition of each member's contribution to the community.

What Can You Do to Support a Child's Response?

1 Encourage them not to be a pushover or not to push others around and to work towards what they want instead.
2 The thoughts we have about ourselves helps. Challenge negative thinking such as 'no one likes me' and promote ideas such as 'my needs count'. Learn not to put ourselves down. Every time you hear a child do this, challenge them with an alternative based on their strengths and special qualities, and remember to model this yourself.

The Kidscape website (www.kidscape.org.uk) has lots of valuable tips for supporting children's assertiveness and offers effective responses to bullying.

Making requests:

- Be clear about what you want
- Plan and practise
- Make your request short (e.g. 'That is mine – I want you to give it back')

The broken record technique:

- Decide what you want to say and stick to it (e.g. 'That's my pencil and I want it back')
- If there is no response, repeat calmly: 'I'm sorry you don't have a pencil, but that's my pencil and I want it back'

Being teased response:

- 'I'm sorry but I didn't hear you' (and repeat if necessary)

Saying 'No':

- We have the right to do this. Listen to what your body and feelings are telling you – what do you really want to say? What do you really want to do?
- If you want to say no, say it early on and first, if possible
- If you are unsure, say you don't know and ask for more time or information
- NO EXCUSES
- Keep walking tall, don't smile and keep good eye contact – practise
- Offer an alternative if you want – remember you are refusing their request and not rejecting them

Fogging:

- Do not respond to insults with insults as this escalates things – fog instead
- Fogging swallows up insults like a great bank of fog (remember saying 'sticks and stones' to yourself?)
- When other people say hurtful things, we can protect ourselves and prevent arguing and getting hurt. We can turn ourselves into fog and swallow up the insults
- If statement is true, say 'That's right'
- If not, we respond 'You could be right' or 'It's possible'
- Keep answers short and bland – the aim is to confuse the bully by responding unexpectedly

Other examples are:

- 'Thank you for that' in response to an insult
- In response to an insult about someone else close to you, say 'That has nothing to do with me'
- Fogging is an alternative to hurt or violence
- Practise. Think about what a bully may say to you and practise – be ready

Other protective approaches:

- Build resilience (see Chapter 10, p.112)
- Increase self-worth
- Encourage children and young people to make their own sound decisions
- Encourage and model good social skills
- Have quality/fun-time as a family – this will also combat stress, and it is very important to combat stress and anxiety
- Activities like swimming and yoga are good for this
- Progressive relaxation techniques are also good – there are plenty of audio-tapes on the market
- Consider other confidence-building activities (e.g. drama or martial arts)

Self-advocacy

As mentioned in earlier chapters, it is very important for the child with SEND to be able to self-advocate, e.g. during person-centred planning activities. The following approach was devised in response to young people with visual impairment (VI) being asked 'What can you see?' by inquisitive peers. They often struggled with how best to respond on the spot and I came up with the idea of writing a ready-made script to help them deal with the situation. Part of the difficulty they experienced was around how to describe their eye condition and this underlined the importance of them being helped to understand their condition as part of their emotional support.

Self-advocacy Through Script-writing: A Guide for Professionals

Young people with VI often get asked 'What can you see?' This can be a problem for them if they are shy, lack confidence or haven't really found a way of explaining to others the nature of their visual experience yet. Some may get upset, assuming that others are being provocative when usually they are interested in learning more about them and maybe in being friends. It can be helpful to both parties to have a script readily available to respond to this sort of enquiry. Casework and personal experience has shown that this can help build mutual trust, dispel embarrassment and even enlist new buddies. It is particularly helpful with young people who have recently acquired sight loss and are going through the adjustment process later in childhood. A similar exercise may help the parents of very young children as the narratives they build may help themselves deal with enquiries from family or neighbours and help them to support their child as they develop.

Writing the Script Using the Example of Retinitis Pigmentosa or Cone-rod Dystrophy

Step 1. About my eye condition

This is an activity that should be facilitated by an adult with knowledge of the child's eye condition or by someone who can guide them in their own research, e.g. through appropriate websites. In order to draft a script, the young person must first have an understanding of their eye condition and the implications of their sight loss for functioning. For example:

'The back of my eye is affected and the parts of the eye that pick up light and detail, e.g. small print, facial expressions or pictures, are affected. Because the rod cells at the back of the eye are dying, I also have difficulty seeing in very bright light or when the lighting level is low, which can mean that I have difficulty getting around in some situations and not others.'

Step 2. Implications for me, my family and friends

This step involves discussing the implications of the child's condition for themselves and others. It may help to select a couple of examples that may have the greatest impact if the young person was to get their point of view over, e.g.'I cannot read normal sized print and need to use large print or Braille. Sometimes, if large print or Braille versions are not available, it is helpful to have people read out to me (e.g. menus) or to use my low vision aids. Also, unless people are very close to me in good light I cannot recognise them so they need to tell me their name when they approach me until I get used to their voice. I need to tell new friends or teachers that this is important to me so that I don't miss something. If a room is dark or if I change from one lighting level to another, it can take time for my eyes to adjust. I sometimes need to use my cane to let others know why they need to not rush past or why I slow up so that I can stay safe.'

Step 3. What do I say when people ask 'What can you see?'

Here you will need to help the young person choose some statements that they will find easy to remember 'on the spot'. Remember, although they may need help with this, it is important to enable them to use their own words. This is important if their explanation is to be understood by the young person and their peer group. The example here is directed at older children but if you are doing this for a younger child, the issues and language used will need to be adapted to the child's developmental level. It can help to prepare a variety of scripts for different situations, e.g. when the young person is in a rush or has more time to explain fully.

Full version 'Well, I have a general impression of things but cannot see little things like small writing and things in the distance. Using computer technology can help with reading. I use low vision aids too, for example hand-held magnifiers or Braille. I can watch a football match if I use a monocular which is a bit like a telescope. It is tiring but worth it sometimes – or I listen to the match instead on the radio. Glasses don't work but there are other ways around some of the things that fully sighted people are able to see. The world is changing and even DVDs now have audio-description, for example.

The reason I carry a cane is to help me find my way around as independently as possible and to let people know to walk around me in busy places. My sight is unreliable, but there are many things that I can do really well.'

Short version 'Well, the reason I carry a cane is because my sight is unreliable, working better sometimes than others. It is to warn people that I may bump into them. Glasses don't work for me. Indoors at home I can whizz around the house as I remember where everything is and I can study well using a PC that makes writing bigger and clearer for me, etc. Thanks for asking. Have a nice day!'

Friendly/funny version 'Well, I have a very hazy picture of the world – a bit like walking around in fog all the time. I need to use my brains and memory more than most for getting around and I use computer technology to help me study, listening to music or playing games. Sometimes these things don't help though, like the time when I accidentally sat on my Dad's lap when the lights were down for the Christmas tree!'

Remember that the scripts will vary with individual functioning and their narrative style. As well as the child's developmental level, it can be useful to rehearse the script (although it does not have to be remembered verbatim) until the person is confident enough to try one out.

Step 4. Rehearse

Now provide an opportunity for the young person to rehearse the script, either with yourself or a trusted friend or member of the family. If you are doing this with a group of young people you could run it as a role play exercise. With an older teenager, you could even run it as a preparation for transition and practise making disability disclosures for job, further education or higher education interviews.

Step 5. Practice

Now encourage the young person to practise using their scripts with trusted friends or members of the family until they feel comfortable.

Step 6. Review

Review the process to see how it worked in a real life situation and adjust as necessary. From time to time ask them whether they have needed to use their script lately and whether it had helped or not.

Summary of Approach

1 About my needs
  Research with the child any implications for functioning academically, mobility wise and socially.
2 Implications for me, my family and friends
  Jot down the effects of the condition together. Remember to use the opportunity to challenge the adversity that the need brings and elicit positive solutions to the negatives raised.
3 Write a full-length version, a short version and a funny version, if possible, so the young person is prepared for different situations.
4 Rehearse.

5   When ready, encourage the child to try using their script when out and about.
6   Review.

Don't forget, this approach can be useful for preparing the child for transition reviews, for dealing with new members of staff or for preparing for other interviews. Appendix 1 (information about the child's needs/condition, p.137–138) may be useful in helping you prepare for this activity.

Effective Person-centred Planning to Address EWB

In Chapter 6 we highlighted how important it is for the child's sense of competence that they are able to engage with tasks and complete them successfully. A full account of how this is delivered by practitioners is outside the scope of this book, but I would not be doing CYPSEND justice if I were not to emphasise the importance of the professionals around them ensuring their success in order to promote self-worth, competence, emotional well-being and motivation. There are resources available that help the practitioner to support autonomy in a lively way, such as 'In the Driving Seat', a toolkit produced by Positive Eye (McCormack, 2011); this company primarily publishes resources and runs courses for practitioners working with children with visual impairments. The same company provides guidance to practitioners in applying quality standards to provision for CYPSEND. By ensuring that a child has access to the curriculum, any specialist equipment needed, adapting the physical environment and considering self-help skills, one is supporting EWB. However, in this chapter we have focused on strategies to enhance emotional competencies.

A further issue to present here is the consideration of what specific emotional needs *may* arise with a SEND so that we can plan objectives and choose suitable programmes to meet any need. These days, evidence-based practice is standard good practice, and I encourage an approach that matches a child's specific needs and objectives to choosing appropriate resources. Of course where an emotional literacy programme is not allowing access, this part of the curriculum needs modification, as with any other (as illustrated earlier in the description of the use of a feelings vocabulary).

We finish the chapter with a table summarising the potential needs that may be evident in a child with SEND and the approaches to be considered at an individual, family and school level (Table 9.1).

Finally, a word on a very practical way of enhancing a child's sense of competency and self-worth. Adults around the child who has an 'I can't do' approach to their work or life can make a huge difference to them by providing them with a responsibility, whether it is giving them the role of trolley monitor at school or helping to feed the animals at home. Such activities also build positive emotions because we all benefit from helping others, as we saw in the first chapter of this book.

Table 9.1 Building emotional competencies in SEND

	Needs	Objectives
Individual level	Low self-worth, stigma	Build self-respect, positive self-identity, strengths recognition and development
	Low self-confidence	Promote self-advocacy
	Anger	Anger management and assertiveness training
	Social skills	Promote awareness of body language techniques (EL resources may require modification and feedback opportunities)
	Anxiety and depression	Promote relaxation techniques and opportunities and seek counselling support to express feelings and build resilience
Family level	Anger, destructive behaviours	Anger management, identifying the trigger factors and sharing with the family to modify behaviours sustaining this response
	Anxiety in family	Encourage use of relaxation techniques, searching for opportunities to have fun together
	Low self-determination, independence	Explore opportunities for learning independence skills and connect with extra-curricular opportunities
	Parental well-being issues	Encourage parents to address their own emotional needs, e.g. are they grieving? (See Chapter 11)
School level	Isolation, lack of participation (relatedness/belonging)	Promote social inclusion and understanding of impact of the SEND, e.g. use of 'circle of friends', awareness-raising training
	Self-efficacy and motivation (competence)	Removal of barriers to accessing the curriculum, e.g. modifying PE, use of ICT
	Confidence and independence (autonomy)	Promotion of real choices and freedom, e.g. by the provision of 'enabling' LSAs who can provide effective and appropriate support

Summary

In this chapter we have covered the following key points.

Child Level

It is important for children:

- to be involved in programme planning and setting their own targets;
- to know their strengths;

(Continued)

(Continued)

- to know how to apply their strengths;
- to be able to adapt emotional literacy programmes to the SEND;
- to have their needs met effectively;
- to recognise when they need to ask for help and to be able to self-advocate;
- to have a sense of keeping pace with their peers and to recognise their accomplishment; to recognise signs of fatigue and emotional lability;
- to acquire new skills as alternatives to other usual methods, e.g. touch typing instead of lagging behind classmates with immature handwriting that is negated by adults and others around the child;
- to be able to undertake positive self-talk.

Family Level

Parents need to:

- acknowledge the child's need for responsibility;
- provide sensitive, responsive parenting;
- be aware of the need for competence and engagement;
- help the child recognise their strengths and apply them to new situations;
- offer feedback about new competencies and problems solved;
- recognise accomplishments and strengths.

School Level

Staff at school need to:

- acknowledge the child's need for responsibility, e.g. so that they can be seen contributing to the school community, hence promoting inclusion;
- offer responsive support so that the child's sense of autonomy is maintained as well as their need to complete work successfully;
- be aware of their need for experiencing competence and engagement to maintain and develop motivation;
- differentiate the PSHE curriculum, e.g. in order to enable the perception of emotions portrayed non-verbally, provide audio-description;
- provide feedback on problems solved, strengths and accomplishments.

10
Towards Belonging

Chapter overview

In this chapter we will look at how to manage children's emotional responses when they are potentially getting in the way of them being included socially or feeling that they belong. We will also look at particular developmental barriers that may prevent social inclusion and what strategies may be put in place to promote positive connections and social skills to offset the potential risk.

We will look at two case studies. The first will show how you may help an older child to cope better with their specific learning difficulties using the STEP model. The second will show how important it is to provide effective partnership support for a young child with Autism Spectrum Disorder (ASD) who is unable to regulate their own emotions. Further key points are made about strategies supportive of belonging at individual, family and school/community level.

Key phrases

Autism Spectrum Disorder (ASD); awareness-raising; dyslexia; emotional regulation; non-verbal gestures; perspective-taking; psycho-social barriers; sensitivity; sensory; parent partnership; social communication; social skills; transitions

The Emotional Response

As mentioned in Chapter 7 (p. 71), the child with SEND sometimes has difficulty coming to terms with uncomfortable feelings related to their needs. They need particular monitoring during or leading up to the outcome of an assessment, during transitions such as class, school or house moves, and through the teenage years when they are trying to assert their independence. Positive emotional support that acknowledges the child's concerns can often help, but where the child's feelings persist, it can help for a child to speak to someone about these issues.

It may help them to see the educational psychologist for the school, or the school counsellor or youth worker. Peer mentors may be able to help too. Specialists working with the child can be a great source of support to pastoral or care staff as they understand the implications of a child's needs for their social and emotional functioning. This is important as adults supporting the child need to know about possible instrumental support that may be necessary to enable the child to find solutions.

In Chapter 9 (p. 95) we looked at how applying a child's strengths and skills in other areas can help them find solutions to situations they find difficult. We will now look at an approach for older children and young people that takes a slightly more structured approach, should the need arise.

The STEP Model

The STEP model approach (based on Seligman's ABCDE approach, 2003) is based on challenging a child's negative thinking where they have become 'stuck' with an adversity. It directs the child away from a focus on what they find difficult to problem-solving ways around the issues using their strengths and other resources around them. It also builds on the self-advocacy skills that we covered in Chapter 9 (p.105).

S = Sense the situation and the emotions behind it

This step is about spotting the situations that exacerbate the adversity that the young person faces. Children with SEND are bombarded constantly by situations that act as barriers to full participation. Some of these are psycho-social, e.g. other people making assumptions about what they can or cannot do. The first step of the process involves considering the situation and why it makes the young person uncomfortable.

T = Try to understand

This step involves examining beliefs about what's going on and perspective-taking, trying to take on board the reasons for the problem. The young person's understanding of their needs or disability and its implications is important here. If negative attributions are being made, the young person needs to consider more positive thinking and recognise that negative thinking is unhelpful.

E = Energise-express yourself and find coping strategies

After accepting the need to find a solution, the young person reflects on strategies that they may use, for example:

- Talking through the issue with a person
- Developing assertiveness
- Applying Anger Management Strategies (e.g. Faupel, Herrick and Sharp, 1998)
- Applying their strengths to the problem concerned
- Relaxing to combat anxiety, doing some exercise.

P = Push forward towards goals

This step involves applying the strategies chosen to the given situation and noting the effect. Encourage the young person to reflect on what went well and consider how taking this step contributes to longer-term goals. Use the opportunity to draw out further strengths that may come to light as a result of going through the process.

If you think that this approach may be helpful to a child you are working with, make sure that you know about the implications of their SEND for their functioning and that you can think of alternative solutions if necessary. You may find it helpful to use the My STEP Forward Worksheet (Appendix 10, p.153) to help with this. Or you may want to work alongside a specialist in the area. The child may be happy to talk to friends or family about their feelings, but if they seem to be having difficulty finding positive ways of looking at their situation, ask if they would like to have counselling support or to meet with the educational psychologist.

Case Study: Siobhan

Siobhan (14) is struggling with her coursework in school. She is thinking of studying textiles at college when she leaves school, but is afraid that she won't get the grades necessary in her core subjects as her dyslexia makes it hard for her to read the texts she will need to study, let alone record her ideas about them. She is cross with her dad because he thinks she is lazy (she is always finding excuses not to complete her homework as she is too tired when she comes home from school) and she is getting concerned that her teachers think she is lazy too. Over the last year, this tension has built up into a lot of stress for her and she has started to self-harm. Her form tutor has noticed the marks on her arms and is increasingly concerned about what is going on.

Point for Reflection

You are Siobhan's form tutor, Ann. How could you use the STEP process to help Siobhan? What happened when you took this approach? Now look at Figure 10.1.

Sense

The form tutor (Ann) sits with S. during the next tutor period and asks her whether there is something on her mind (she knows that SIB is a sign of stress). S. explains that she is tired of struggling with her dyslexia and the way people treat her because of it. Ann doesn't know much about dyslexia so asks S. to explain how it affects her but S. is unable to explain except to say that she is fed up with getting red ink all over her work, being asked to read out in class and running out of time to write down her homework properly. Ann suspects that these feelings have affected S.'s self-confidence and her ability to explain these feelings to adults. She also knows that she may get into trouble for making excuses or refusing to do certain things.

She thanks Siobhan for explaining how she feels and asks if it would be OK to find out more about how her dyslexia affects her from the SENCO and arranges to see S. later in the week for another chat.

Meanwhile Ann finds out about the implications of S.'s dyslexia for herself and for others from the SENCO.

(Continued)

(Continued)

Try to understand

When they meet again, Ann does some perspective-taking work with Siobhan, asking her, first of all, what does her dad know about her dyslexia? S. realises that Dad was not at the appointment with the specialist teacher when she was 8 when her mum was told about dyslexia and what it was going to mean for her (including how tired she could get after a day in school). She realises too that her mum and dad are both working hard for their family and have little time to help with homework.

Together they put down a short list of the main difficulties S. has because of her dyslexia and the strategies that the SENCO explained to Ann that may help. S. liked some of the suggestions but thinks that all her teachers need to know about them too. (Ann decided to discuss this with the SENCO who she knows has been trying to share the information with S.'s subject teachers.) Also, one of the suggestions: learning to touch type so that S. can use a laptop to record her course work had been refused by S. Further discussion revealed that S. was worried that the other students would be jealous about her having a laptop and that she didn't want to be bullied.

Realising that S. had a review of her needs coming up, she encouraged S. to ask her parents if she could talk to them about her feelings about her dyslexia and come back to her with some ideas to solve the problems.

Energise

Siobhan came up with some really good ideas for sorting the problems out:

- To practise what she is going to say if people ask 'why have you got a laptop?' For example, acknowledging that she is grateful to have it because it stops her having to write things out over and over again before she can get it good enough to hand in.
- Her mum reminded her that she has a really good memory for visual things so would learn the keyboard quickly. Siobhan decided to ask if she could have touch typing lessons at the next review.
- When she talked to dad about how cross she was about being accused of being lazy she also told him about what her day was like and how she had to re-do a lot of her work. (Amazingly to her) he understood and they agreed a time for her to do her homework after she had had a break. He even offered to help her use the dictionary on the family PC so that she could check her work.
- She asked if it would be OK to carry round a laminated card with brief dos and don'ts for her teachers, e.g. 'Please don't ask me to read out in front of everyone'.

Ann took her ideas to the SENCO ready for the next review and encouraged S. to ask for help with the ideas at the review. Dad was especially invited to the next review to ensure that he could see how hard she had been working and to find out more ways of helping her now that she is 14.

Push forward

At the review of her needs, Siobhan asked if she could learn to touch type after all, and whether the SENCO could help her design a fun, polite way of reminding her teachers about her special needs.

A list of her new coping strategies was drawn up so that everyone around Siobhan could encourage her to use them and focus on how these small steps were going to help with her future.

It was clear that she had a lot of strengths that she could use to help her make further progress.

Everyone agreed that she had been working hard and that she needed help to have more fun and relaxation to help with her stress and tiredness.

Targets were set with Siobhan so that she knew what to look for when she was successful. At last she could see that college was a real possibility for the first time.

Figure 10.1   Example of a completed STEP worksheet for Siobhan

Point for Reflection

What steps were taken to increase Siobhan's autonomy, competence and sense of belonging? Why did she need to learn to be a little more assertive? How did her form tutor help her with her emotional literacy?

A suggested answer is as follows. By encouraging Siobhan to think up her own ideas for solving her problems and talking with her parents, she was put in the position of accepting that there was something that needed to be addressed and that it was in her power to do so. Talking with her form tutor and parents helped to develop her understanding of her feelings and led to better ways of managing them. In particular, her form tutor was well aware that teenagers often have difficulty with perspective-taking and asking her to put herself in dad's shoes may well have led to a breakthrough. Asking dad to come to her SEN review then enabled him to see her side of the issues (adults can sometimes give up trying to do this with teenagers when communication breaks down). These strategies helped her with her sense of autonomy and belonging as well as improving her emotional literacy. Accepting the need to learn a new skill to offset her frustrations with her written work will also increase her sense of competence and control over her needs. The best thing of all, for me as a psychologist, was to see that by agreeing to realistic plans and targets, we restored hope and optimism for the future.

The solutions described above were both affective and instrumental and illustrate good partnership working. Although children need to develop coping strategies as they get older, they need scaffolding to do so. They need others around them to empathise and perspective-take as well as having to learn this essential social skill themselves. (Please see the photocopiable My STEP Forward Worksheet provided in Appendix 10 for your use.)

Building Connections

In the next case study, we will look at the emotional needs of children with ASD. These children face a particular challenge as they lack the ability to empathise with others and therefore find the social world around them a confusing and often scary place.

Case Study: Ashraf

Ashraf (3) was a very placid and well-behaved baby. His mother found him very easy to care for compared with her four other children until he started nursery class. She thought that he was slow to pick up speech and self-care skills, but that going to a nursery would help with this, and found it quicker to do most things for him. She thought he was more anxious than the others when they started school but thought that the tantrums on arrival to nursery would pass (and so did his teacher). A settling-in period was agreed to give him a chance to get used to his new routines. Unfortunately, an early review had to be called because he had been biting another child in the class and this child's mother had asked for Ashraf to be removed from the nursery. At this point the teacher in charge asked permission from Ashraf's mum for him to be assessed by an educational psychologist.

Observations and assessments led to some management strategies and further assessments by a speech and language therapist and community paediatrician as he seemed to be extremely sensitive to certain noises, such as water taps running, and did not seem to follow verbal instructions in the group setting. After extensive multi-disciplinary assessment, it was concluded that his developmental disorder was autism. Strategies were put in place, such as visual timetables to help him make sense of the new rules and routines in the nursery. In fact, this helped a number of other children too. Staff members learned how to remove Ashraf from certain situations before he became too upset and aggressive, leading him to an area of the room which was set aside for calming activities such as looking at picture books (which he loved). Ashraf's mum was introduced to the 'social stories' approach to help introduce him to more self-help skills, such as turning the water tap on by himself when washing. A home–school diary was also set up to share strategies that worked and to ensure consistent management which helped Ashraf deal with the environmental changes and people better.

Social Communication and Emotional Regulation

Children with ASD have a hard time – not only do other adults see them as challenging in their behaviour, but they can make all sorts of assumptions about a parent's coping mechanisms and parenting style. Ashraf's case helps to illustrate how his lack of social understanding and sensory integration difficulties prompted an emotional melt-down on entry to nursery. Other parents may assume that he is just a badly behaved child with a poor parent and a teacher who does not manage her class well – thus elevating anxiety and emotional reactions all round.

In the UK in recent years, much has been done to raise awareness of the difficulties that people with ASD face, but stakeholder consultations (e.g. Department of Health, 2009) highlight the need for far more training and awareness-raising among the general public. Such children are challenged by their environment and with the right sort of help from those around the child, not only does their behaviour become less challenging (an outward expression of distress), but the child can be helped to calm down and start to learn alternative means of communication and enjoy their childhood.

In order to include Ashraf on entry to school, it was necessary to observe where barriers to participation were – in this case, his inability to communicate his distress and his sensory sensitivity to certain sounds. Only by augmenting communication and managing his environment was it possible to restore calm to an escalating situation. This strategy also helped Ashraf and his family.

Timely multi-agency assessment and effective programmes are critical to early intervention and improving outcomes for children like Ashraf. Unfortunately, far too many children are removed from school before they get the right sort of help. This can exacerbate their feeling of distress next time they enter a new setting.

Social Skills and Social Stories

Another potential barrier to social inclusion and a sense of belonging is a lack of social skills. There are many social skills programmes available for children across the age range but, as mentioned in Chapters 6 and 7, it is important to choose activities that meet your objective for a child and to modify them as appropriate. For example, a quiz designed to teach the meaning of non-verbal gesture by getting students to act out body language gesture will only engage the class completely if you ensure that a narrator takes on the role of describing the posture adopted for those with a visual impairment.

In Chapter 7 (p. 79), I mentioned the Children's Social Behaviour programme devised by The University of Sussex and Brighton and Hove Council (Banerjee et al., 2004). This programme involved the presentation of cards displaying social situations to young children (7–11 years of age) where they had to discuss among themselves what should happen next. Such an approach is appropriate because it taps into the child's language level rather than being a direct instruction from an adult. It also encourages the use of a feelings vocabulary and problem-solving skills, promoting co-operative behaviour and emotional literacy skills. Again, if the presentation is to be multi-sensory and inclusive, I would advocate the use of a narrator to describe in detail the scene set before the children. This approach also encourages children to consider each other's perspectives, which is important for the development of empathy.

For some children, such as Ashraf, empathy is part of their set of needs. They lack the biological basis for this and some argue that a person with ASD can never truly see other people's perspectives. However, they can learn how to respond in given situations. This skill, sometimes called social cognition, can be taught through strategies such as 'the social use of language' and 'social stories', both of which are now widely used in our schools. Originally developed by Carol Gray for use with children with ASD (Gray, 2000), these programmes are now being widely used with children who lack empathy (perhaps as a result of 'another special need' or because they have experienced environmental barriers to acquiring the skill, such as early neglect or abuse). The approach involves the presentation of an issue causing a difficulty, e.g. 'Why must I put my hand up in class?' The teacher/practitioner describes the situation in which the activity occurs before offering explicit explanations to the child as to why other people do the activity. This is then 'normalised', to ensure that the child accepts the approach as OK, before a couple of directive sentences are used to explaining what they should do next time the need to do the activity arises. In this case, the barrier to 'belonging' is removed by communicating to the child in clear, unambiguous terms (perhaps supplemented by photos or cartoons) what is expected of them. Children with delayed or disordered language often have difficulty with ambiguity so it is important to remove this sort of confusion. By spelling out why other people do the activity, the social rule is demystified, making the situation less threatening.

In my experience, when parents and practitioners help children to write their own social stories, it can help to lower the child's feelings of anxiety. They are less likely to become difficult to manage because, with practice, they learn to anticipate more and more social rules. SEN teachers like them so much when they have tried them out that they start to use them quite widely to help with the management of a range of routines in the class, especially in the early years. A useful resource from this point of view, as it is organised into themes around self-help skills, is Ling (2010). Self-help skills are another potential barrier towards belonging if there is a delay in this area due to a learning disability. As a child develops, acquiring age-appropriate self-help skills is also good for independence and self-determination.

Points for Practice to Promote Belonging

In this chapter we have covered the following key points for promoting belonging.

Child level

- All children need to spend quality time with their family but the child with SEND may be more dependent on their family than most, so this is to be actively encouraged. This builds stronger binds (and therefore security from which to build other friendships), creates opportunities for positive emotions and provides opportunities for feedback about the social world.
- Opportunities for socialising with peers need to be actively sought.
- Where a child has a special need or disability that acts as a barrier to social skills development, modifications to social skills programmes need to be sought to enable participation in these programmes as with any other part of the curriculum.
- Where a child has a need in the area of social understanding and empathy, programmes to promote social communication should be trialled, bearing in mind whether the child can work well in a group or not. For example, where a child has difficulty feeling at ease in a group situation,

activities should be introduced on an individual basis, then upgrading to a group of two others, three others, etc.

- Adults working with the child should actively seek out opportunities in social situations for building self-confidence, etc. Competencies to help them do this, such as self-advocacy skills, need to be built in if necessary.

Family level

- Families need to consider how they provide support to their child. Is it enabling support that is patient, responsive and sensitive to their child's needs? (See Chapter 11, p. 123, for further information.)
- Families need to build in quality time with the child on a daily basis.
- Families need to provide opportunities for unstructured social activities, such as trips to the park.
- In the early years, families are especially important for giving feedback about the social environment and, as the child gets older, about appearance, etc. The emphasis should be on unconditional positive regard rather than criticism.
- Reinforcement by parents of age-appropriate social skills is important. Gaining attention for good behaviour is preferable to a child having to draw attention through misbehaviour. If a behaviour is unacceptable, the family needs to condemn the act, not the person (to protect self-worth and build appropriate behaviours).
- All members of the family need to understand the implications of a child's disability in order to provide further support in promoting self-advocacy as the child develops. It is also important for siblings to understand so that they can explain to others about their brother or sister's difficulties.
- Parents need to be actively involved in programmes to address difficulties surrounding social communication so that they can reinforce the strategies in natural settings. Parental partnership in general is to be actively encouraged. This aspect is more difficult to achieve in larger school settings but some schools get around this by providing workshops on behaviour for parents.
- In the home situation it is possible to provide opportunities for personal responsibility and developing a team/group working ethic. Children love being given responsibility and getting recognition for it, and it takes some of the strain off the parent too!

School level

- School has a very important role to play in managing the provision of opportunities for unstructured social activities. Zoned areas in playgrounds are increasingly being introduced in recognition of children's different needs and preferences. There is no need these days for team sports to dominate the play opportunities for children. Some children find boisterous play more threatening because of their physical condition. Some are unable to take part because they have a difficulty in understanding turn-taking, group rules, etc. Creative management of the playground is important to optimise access to play for all children.
- As children grow and develop, feedback from the peer group about social rules and appearance becomes more important than the influence of family. Extra-curricular activities organised at school need to be as accessible as possible to allow children with SEND to have the same opportunities as other children.

(Continued)

(Continued)

- Reinforcement of age-appropriate social skills is a major role for schools and the selection of appropriate resources and providing access to them is important. Useful guidelines are available to help schools promote social and emotional literacy and social skills (e.g. Faupel, 2003; Weare, 2004; Rae, 2007). Of course, the Social and Emotional Aspects of Learning (SEAL) curriculum (DCSF, 2008) has now been widely introduced across the age range in the UK too. In all cases, it is important to match activities to the objective identified in the pupil/s' individual education plan and that children and parents are actively engaged (see Shotton, 2009, for examples of pupil-friendly resources). Again, please note the need to adapt or modify resources to ensure accessibility.
- Schools are helping to identify increasing numbers of children with social communication difficulties and children are often provided with programmes to address this. However, there is also a need to raise awareness and provide training for practitioners in how to help a child manage this need in a social context and how practitioners themselves should respond. For example, a child with ASD who has a difficulty with queuing should not be expected to queue in the dining room at lunch-time. Also, assemblies can be used to raise awareness of such issues as well as to celebrate diversity and challenge negative stereotyping by providing examples of positive role models to young people, such as famous people with SEN, etc. Specialists, such as educational psychologists and speech therapists, who regularly visit the school, may help with training. Social inclusion is a two-way process involving changes in behaviour by people around the child. Greater understanding of SEND is necessary if the child is not to be simply assimilated into a non-disabled social environment.
- Schools need to enable personal responsibility and develop team and group work.
- Schools need to apply safeguarding practices.
- Schools need to promote inclusive practices and awareness-raising activities in the peer group, and combine these with Circle of Friends approaches (Frederickson et al., 2005; and see Inclusive Solutions, www.inclusive-solutions.com), a company that provides practical solutions and ideas to promote effective inclusion in mainstream schools, early years settings and communities. Circle of Friends is an approach to building the inclusion, in a mainstream setting, of any young person (known as 'the focus child'), who is experiencing difficulties in school because of a disability, personal difficulties or because of their challenging behaviour towards others. The approach works by raising awareness in the young person's peers to enable them to provide support and engage in problem solving with the young person in difficulty.
- Remember to seek the permission of the focus child, the pastoral care staff and the parents of the child to put such an approach in place.

Summary

In this chapter we have covered the following key points:

Child Level

It is important for children:

- to come to terms with feelings related to their needs;
- to develop their social and emotional skills to enable them to make strong connections that can offset isolation;

- to have a strong bond with their family to provide their security and capacity for establishing friendships;
- to have opportunities for practising their social skills.

Family Level

It is important for the family:

- to provide positive, enabling support to help their child build their security and confidence to build social connections;
- to provide warmth and empathy for the child's needs;
- to provide structured and unstructured opportunities for practising their social skills as the child develops;
- to provide clear boundaries and feedback to their child about the social world;
- to work in partnership with their child's school to enable reinforcement of strategies designed to enhance social competence.

School Level

It is important for schools to:

- differentiate the personal and social curriculum for children with SEND just as they would for the academic elements of the curriculum;
- consider strategies to mentor the child with SEND in coming to terms with emotional responses to their needs. Implementing these may help offset a prolonged reaction that may lead to social exclusion;
- to work with other agencies such as speech and language therapists and educational psychologists where the child concerned has social communication needs;
- to work in partnership with parents to help reinforce newly acquired skills in the home setting.

11
A Guide for Parents

Chapter overview

In this chapter we will look at the specific emotional needs of children and young people with SEND and their parents. The chapter is also written with teaching assistants in mind as they also have a caring role and are key professionals in nurturing the child's development and independence. All children need to develop a strong bond with a caregiver, a shared understanding of the world, and growing independence. We will examine how the parents of children with SEND can encourage the development of these essential building blocks for emotional well-being.

This chapter may be copied and shared with parents to help explain the approach that is being taken to proactively support emotional well-being in their child. It follows the main structure of the book:

- The introduction of autonomy or independence in the early and teenage years;
- Optimising the child's sense of competence or capability (again in the early years and teens);
- Promoting friendships and social inclusion across the age range.

The chapter concludes with guidance on the recognition and development of personal qualities and strengths from a young age to help with transition planning.

Key phrases

Anxiety; attachment; cognitive change strategies; controllability; fatigue; feedback; grief reaction; mediating approaches; motivation; partnership working; positive emotions; self-determination; shared attention; social and emotional development

The Emotional Impact of Having a Child with a SEND

We will start this chapter by acknowledging the challenges that parenting a child with SEND brings. Most parents would describe rearing all children as joyful trouble. However, there are additional issues for parents of children and young people with disabilities. For example, there may be initial trauma, e.g. unexpected birth complications or an accident, or there may be difficulty coping with family and friends' responses to the news of the child's SEND.

Attitudes Towards Disability

This is closely linked to acceptance of disability in adults so it is important to be aware of how you feel about your child living with a SEND. Do you feel scared of the future? Why? Do you need to find out more about the implications of the condition and the ways people find around it? It can help to talk with others who understand what you are going through.

Often parents will express that they have not told friends or family about the diagnosis. This may be difficult when you are trying to work out your own attitudes, perhaps having to challenge your own assumptions for your child's future. Having someone to listen to you, being non-judgemental and setting modest goals are important ways of coping in the early days and through transitions. Ask your child's school for suggestions as to locally available support for parents, e.g. educational psychologists, family support teams, etc.

In order to respond to such issues, it helps to understand the nature and implications of the child's difficulties in an informed way. Hopefully, parents will have had the opportunity to ask about these issues at the point of diagnosis or at the review of their child's needs. A good resource for parents is the Contact a Family website (www.cafamily.org.uk), which provides details of over 1,000 medical conditions and provides useful links to parents' support groups and organisations specialising in the condition. Knowledge and coping skills are essential to handling adjustment to SEND and gathering in information about the condition is an important first step. Until you understand the implications of a child's condition it is difficult to anticipate how it will affect them in their day-to-day lives. You should bear in mind, though, that each child is unique. Each child will have varying degrees of the condition/s and live in environments and attend schools that vary enormously. This is where it is possible to manage things to optimise the child's learning and life opportunities, and finding out what support is available locally is key to helping you with this.

Some parents have a grief reaction to the news that their child has a SEND. This is natural and different members of a family may grieve in different ways and at different rates. Over the years, I have had individual members of a couple confide in me their concern that the other partner is over-reacting or burying their head in work and distancing themselves. There is no absolute here, other than the need for tolerance, mutual respect and the need for time to come to terms with your feelings. It can take months or even years to restructure life following a diagnosis involving complex medical needs, but the strength of the feeling of loss will diminish with time.

Some parents become extremely anxious about the future that may be in front of their child. It is difficult to live with uncertainty at the best of times, but when you have little experience or knowledge of the child's condition, that uncertainty can become all the greater. The voluntary sector can often help in this respect, as they have experience of supporting parents, e.g. by sharing examples of helpful approaches. This can restore hope and instil meaning and purpose in what it is you need to do as a parent.

Professionals working with your child should also be able to listen and support you, and challenge any assumptions that you may have (understandably) made about the future. Initially, parents can feel very isolated and alone as they begin to come to terms with what has happened to their child. In the early days, it may help to know that it is natural to feel disbelief or guilt and anger but that, given time, most people adapt successfully and begin to accept what has happened.

Cognitive change strategies such as the ABCDE strategy (Seligman, 2003) can be useful if unhelpful beliefs persist in the longer term. It is important to address unresolved emotional issues as a negative parental emotional reaction may result in an aggressive response in the child as they develop. This can lead to additional stress.

- A – Adversity. What are you faced with?
- B – Beliefs. What beliefs do you hold about that adversity?
- C – Consequences. What are the consequences of holding on to those beliefs? Are the beliefs helpful or unhelpful to the child?
- D – Disputation. If the beliefs are unhelpful and persistent, e.g. why my child?, you need to set about gathering information and getting facts about the implications of the condition to challenge your beliefs. Simply knowing more about technological solutions or medical advances may help, but if you become 'stuck' with this it is advisable to seek professional help and ask your GP or other key workers about any support that may be available locally for you.
- E – Energisation. Having discovered that there are strategies that you can put in place to help, set about planning how to access them. For example, make arrangements to visit the hydrotherapy pool with your child to reinforce the exercises that the physiotherapist recommends.

Some parents find themselves getting very frustrated by the system which is supposed to be supporting their child. If this happens, it may help to speak to someone who is impartial or to seek further information from one of the resources listed at the end of this chapter.

Parental Mental Health and Other Family Issues

It is common to feel an overwhelming sense of grief about your child's SEND – it can feel like a real sense of bereavement. Individuals vary in their response, but people often feel sadness, disbelief, anger and uncertainty. It is important to share these feelings with people you trust, but containment of these feelings is also important in supporting your child. Some children hold back their own feelings because they do not want to worry their parents and they need their parents to be strong. If you are having difficulties, especially if the feelings persist, it is important to see your GP or seek emotional support.

Some people suffer prolonged periods of psychological distress in response to a diagnosis. They may need more intensive help, such as cognitive behaviour therapy, if they have difficulty changing negative beliefs. They may also have pre-existing conditions which are exacerbated by the additional stress of coming to terms with a child's SEND, or family relationships may already be dysfunctional. If you think that you are experiencing these scenarios, it is important to seek help from your GP in the first instance.

Professionals can help by sharing knowledge and experience about the implications of SEND in the areas discussed in this chapter. It is important to be aware that threats to the stability and security of the child can arouse anxiety, so strategies for managing this anxiety are crucial. Increased care-giving demands, e.g. managing appointments, educational issues, etc., can take their toll. Few people are aware of, let alone understand, the additional strain of caring for and about a child with SEND. I am constantly impressed with the way that families learn to cope, especially as so many also manage to find time for fun – which is essential for offsetting anxiety.

Point for Practice

You can help your child by:

- making time for yourself to take some exercise or to share time with friends where you can experience a good belly-laugh from time to time;
- building time into family routines for a good laugh together, or days out, or planning breaks away;
- seeking extra support and help from the social care services, especially if you are caring for your child on a 24/7 basis and if you do not have your extended family nearby. It is not giving up to seek respite for an evening a week to spend time with you partner or other children. You need it and deserve it, and it will help your child because you will be refreshed and energised.

Other issues that parents report include:

- difficulties in meeting the needs of non-disabled children;
- stress in meeting the conflicting needs of children;
- older children missing out on attention and 'normal' family activities.

Just as parents need support, there is a need for other members of the family to share their experiences and emotions with others in the same situation.

The Emotional Development of Your Child

Attachment

A good bond between a parent and their child is essential to long-term mental health. It protects against life's challenges and promotes a person's ability to make and sustain friendships. A good parenting relationship involves a subtle responsiveness to your child, where you intervene whenever your child makes a sign of some kind. In the early years, 'scaffolding' or mediating approaches are useful. These approaches are commonly used by teachers of young children and by responsive parents. They involve observing a child and spotting signs that they are beginning to struggle. The adult then puts in suggestions or actions that actively encourage the child to take the next step. For example, if your child is solving a jigsaw puzzle and they keep coming back to the same piece but in the wrong orientation, you might rotate the piece so that they can recognise that it may fit into the gap now that it has been rotated. Of course you may have to repeat such actions many times for some children, but they are more likely to learn to manipulate pieces in the future to solve a problem than if you do the awkward bits for them. It may be necessary to learn to use other pathways to building the usual skills, e.g. using tactile or visual means when a child has a hearing difficulty.

If a child does not give eye contact early on, a sighted parent can find bonding difficult. However, you can develop a close bond with your child by using your voice to replace reassuring looks and smiles. Likewise, gentle touch can communicate so much. Baby massage helps some parents establish a responsive bond.

This shared attention is important in establishing a bond but it is also important for the development of empathy in your child, which is vital for their social and emotional development. If your child is not giving you much eye contact or is not looking in the direction where you are pointing (but is rather looking at the end of your finger) by 18 months old, have a chat to your health visitor or paediatrician if your child is under review. You can help to address this by applying the strategies above and by talking about or showing your child the objects that are common to your family routines and explaining why you all use or do these things.

As a parent, it can be difficult to get the balance right between giving your child too much and too little attention. Over-attentiveness may lead to poor motivation as the child does not learn to handle little challenges or disappointments. It may also lead to anxiety. Therefore, over-zealous parenting has its downside and needs to be addressed! It is kinder to your child in the longer term even though it can seem harsh at the time. It is fine to give your child pointers or clues as to how to do their homework, but it is inadvisable to do it for them. Believe it or not, this is sometimes what happens. If your child is unable to complete the homework that has been set, it is important to check whether the work set is accessible to them. Teachers like to have feedback about concerns like this – it helps them to meet the needs of your child. The gold standard is to be able to work in partnership.

Conversely, neglectful, unresponsive parenting will undermine development as the child with a SEND may rely more heavily on feedback about the world around them. It may also be a sign of rejection or stress in the family. Both issues need to be resolved. If you are experiencing difficulty in this area, talk to your GP. Referral to a specialist health visitor, or a clinical or educational psychologist may be appropriate. (See Chapter 7, p. 73, for examples of acceptance behaviours that parents may show towards their child.)

Independence

Controllability

As we have seen through the rehabilitation literature in earlier chapters, self-efficacy and locus of control are important factors underpinning adjustment. The introduction of new or alternative skills or the replacement of lost skills to enhance competence and autonomy are important factors here. A family's attitude towards the use of aids is important as well as their socio-economic status in being able to provide resources or to access the benefit system to find support, resources and help.

Dependency Versus Control

It is important to recognise the tension between dependency and control in coming to terms with SEND. We all need to feel loved and interdependent, but we also need varying degrees of autonomy and control over our environment (Wilson, 2003). Family relationships are central to how we experience attachment and dependence as well as the quality of the support that is necessary to enable self-efficacy.

Early Years

It can be hard to see your child struggle with tasks and the desire to do things for them can be overwhelming. But it is important for your child to develop persistence and determination, as this supports the motivation your child needs to succeed. Let your child have a go at lots of tasks, and only intervene when they show outward signs of needing help (perhaps turning towards you). A responsive parent can let a child try to get dressed, for example (to begin with, this may involve just letting them do the last bit). Provide opportunities for them to make real choices so your child develops confidence in making informed decisions. Offering praise and describing how you are doing something helps too.

Teenage Years

Young people aged 14–16 need a range of self-help skills. Research tells us that young people with disabilities often have fewer opportunities to develop necessary free choice skills. Sometimes, in an attentive, caring family, a child may have had everything done for them and have become very dependent on adults or others. Some are happy with this and some are not, as they become increasingly aware of their peers being allowed greater choice and control as they develop. The young person needs to develop confidence in acquiring life skills and in decision-making in preparation for adult life. Allowing them greater autonomy gradually does this, and it may also make the atmosphere at home better.

If you have only recently recognised tensions or the need to address this question of independence, you'll need to put a plan in place to allow greater autonomy in a safe way. This is another time when it can be helpful to appraise what your child can and cannot do in terms of self-help skills. In my experience, when a child with SEND goes on their first school trip they are often surprised at what they can do for themselves, if they are sharing the same experiences with their peers. Of course, some will still need sensitive, effective support at hand to help manage certain situations in a dignified way (e.g. showering). From approximately age 14 onwards, it is important to involve social care services in the planning of self-care in preparation for adulthood. If your child has a significant level of need this may already be in place, but if not, have a word with your GP or SENCO about how to access support with this. You need to feel confident about letting them go into town safely with their friends, for example, and some input from a mobility specialist or problem-solving around their organisational skills may make all the difference.

Coping with Increased Demands and/or Stress

Never underestimate the additional time and organisational demands of making sure that your child's needs are met. It impacts on the whole family and that's before we even consider the pragmatics of everyday life when there are adjustments to be made to compensate for a loss of functioning. It is important for you and your family to offset this stress by having fun together. It is allowed and the experience of positive emotions can help everyone concerned. The preservation of the family's goals (e.g. planning holidays), social support networks and stress management strategies are crucial in minimising the negative impact of anxiety and fatigue.

Managing Conflict and/or Anger

This is a common problem in the teenage years. Like all children, young people with SEND are establishing their own identity and independence as they approach adulthood. If your child has been very dependent on you, they may become acutely aware of this and start pushing boundaries. While it is important for them to experience real choices and self-determination (independence, a sense of competence and belonging to the peer group/community), it can be hard for a parent to let go, especially if you are concerned about their vulnerability due to their SEND. It is very important at this stage to work in partnership with other professionals who know your child's capabilities to give you feedback about how to 'let go' in small steps and confidently.

If aggression has escalated, there may be trigger factors involved. They often hinge on the implication of the SEND for functioning. Encourage problem-solving as a family around the issue, to try to avoid the trigger presenting. This may mean some awareness-raising in a non-empathic family member. There are many self-help guides in anger management available so ask pastoral staff or your SENCO for an example.

Capability

Feedback, Language Development and Social and Emotional Development in the Early Years

Earlier in this book, in Chapter 7, giving feedback to the young person (e.g. about facial expressions, appearance, etc.) was mentioned as being important to the development of social and emotional literacy. There is a pivotal role here for parents. It is not unkind to spell out what is happening in the social world around the child as you will be helping your child with their socialisation and acceptance by the peer group. Feedback about good posture may even help avoid a bad back or cricked neck later on, or help them to walk or act tall and see off potential bullies.

Children with SEND may receive less feedback from the world around them if they have restricted opportunities for socialising and they rely on their parents more as a result. It is important to describe what is going on in the environment, so your child gets as full a picture as possible. At bath time, for example, you might explain 'In our family we all take a bath so that we smell fresh and feel clean. We have to turn the taps on to make the water run into the bath. It makes a lot of noise but that's OK...'. Some family members need support to develop these 'commentary' skills. Description develops your child's knowledge and vocabulary, but also allays potential anxiety and helps your child to develop a shared understanding of the world. This is essential for social and emotional development.

If your child is not able to see gestures, facial expressions and body language, label emotions so that your child can begin to understand social behaviour and express their own feelings. Explain why another child is smiling broadly, or looking worried, tired or angry, so that your child gradually understands that their own body language communicates their feelings to others. Developing a 'feelings vocabulary' will help your child's ability to manage their feelings in ways that are helpful to others and themselves.

Self-determination

As students get older, encourage your young person to go on school outings and trips so that they have opportunities for making real choices and acquire those vital self-determination skills. This provides your child with opportunities to practise social and emotional competencies as well as to apply self-help skills and decision-making. Such skills are all important components of a child's sense of keeping pace with their peers and capability.

You may need to seek out accessible sporting or leisure activities locally so that teenagers can meet their friends to engage in extra-curricular activities. Most local authorities now have a sports development officer for those with disabilities and they should be able to help you make choices with your child about the opportunities out there.

Academic Competence

It is increasingly recognised that parents have an important role to play in reinforcing educational attainment and policy is being extended to strengthen a parent's entitlement in this area.

In terms of proactively supporting emotional well-being, it is important that the child's educational needs are being met and you have an important role in monitoring this. Essentially, the removal of barriers to being able to access the curriculum is the responsibility of professionals working with the child, but you can help by sharing feedback about patterns of strengths and difficulties and how engaged they are with various aspects of their learning. If a child is avoiding doing homework or seems to be giving up easily, it is a sign that the work is too challenging and that the child's work needs to be more carefully broken down into achievable steps so that they can enjoy a sense of accomplishment. Everyone needs to feel successful if they are to be motivated to continue to put the effort in. Would you continue going to Salsa class if the instructor was not spotting that you were not keeping up and giving a few interim tips as to how to achieve a certain sequence?

In terms of measuring progress, both you and your child need to be involved in setting achievable targets and knowing when they are to be reviewed. This helps everyone's engagement in the process of support.

Fatigue

Some children have to apply a range of alternative coping strategies to compensate for their SEND. For example, a child with Specific Learning Difficulties or dyslexia may break down long words into smaller chunks, rehearse them before recording them and checking them in a dictionary or thesaurus. Not only is this time-consuming, but it draws more heavily on memory and organisational skills than if they did not have that need. You will begin to see how doing this all day in school may lead to fatigue.

Your child may become irritable as a result and slow to get started on homework. One cannot assume that a young person recognises this tiredness or knows how to express the emotions arising from these physical affects. Therefore, you may think they are being lazy or that they are in a mood with you. It is worth encouraging such children to verbalise when they are tired and provide them with options as to how they may refresh themselves prior to completing some more work. Of course it is important that they do not learn to make an excuse of their SEND, but more than anything they need your understanding, approval and support as a parent to help them with this. I have seen this sort of difficulty escalate into family relationship difficulties due to a lack of perspective-taking on both sides. Remember that adults need to manage their emotions too, especially if you expect your child to come to you for guidance and support when they are in real trouble.

Helping your child to recognise fatigue and to address it by telling others when necessary can help relationships, especially in the lead-up to examinations where everyone feels the pressure.

Friendships and Social Inclusion

Getting the balance right between taking care, being responsive, supervising and allowing the child freedom to make real choices, exercise control, and so on is a tough call for most parents. However, when your child is necessarily more dependent, e.g. because of a deterioration in their condition, this equilibrium can be upset, resulting in emotional responses in all concerned. As mentioned earlier, anxiety and anger are common issues arising as parties struggle to adapt to the situation as safely as possible.

Later Childhood or Adolescence

A young person who experiences a SEND suddenly in adolescence may experience a deep sense of loss as a result of losing skills such as reading or socialising freely. In the adjustment phase, they will need the kind of patience and caring normally given to someone who has been bereaved. However, they also need carers who can provide positive support, guiding them towards future plans. You can help your child. Find out more about their condition and the many ways of getting around problems. For example, you can explore aids and technological solutions, and discover role models of people who have gone through such periods of adjustment successfully, as most do. Encourage them to recognise their enduring personality traits and characteristics and help them to develop these strengths by applying them to new situations. Encourage them and provide practical support to them to sustain or develop new friendships.

If you think they lack the social skills necessary to get along in friendships, talk to the SENCO at school. Most schools are now offering personal and social education programmes and emotional literacy support for children with specific emotional development concerns. Such parts of the curriculum are readily adapted for children with SEND, as with any other aspect of the curriculum.

If your child has social communication difficulties such as Autism Spectrum Disorder, you may be asked to practise certain strategies at home to help your child generalise the new skills (e.g. social stories (Gray, 2000)).

Self-confidence and a sense of identity are issues for most teenagers. It is important for your child to keep in touch with at least one trusted friend, who they can rely on when out and about – when choosing clothes, for example. It may be necessary to explain to friends where help is needed (checking bus timetables, prices, how to guide safely, etc.).

Maintaining friendships is important for reducing initial isolation. Also, quality time as a family helps to keep channels of communication open. The chance to relax and have fun offsets anxiety – it is all too easy to forget this when faced with adversity. Children with SEND value people around them offering patient, positive support and being hopeful for the future.

One of the key contributions that a family can make towards their child's adjustment is to provide feedback about their personal qualities and strengths. It is important for them to be able to recognise and develop these strengths so that they are able to self-advocate, e.g. when programme-planning or during transitions to college or work. From an adjustment point of view, it is important to accept the difficulties your child may have, but even more important is to remember that your child has other qualities that may be used to solve problems or to enjoy life and build success.

By applying Martin Seligman's PERMA model (Seligman, 2011), you can check whether all members of your family have the opportunity to flourish, by ensuring that each member has the chance to experience positive emotions, engagement (with schoolwork, other work or hobbies), positive relationships, a sense of meaning and purpose (e.g. hopes for the future), and a sense of accomplishment.

Case Study: Kai

Kai is a disaffected teenager with a working memory difficulty that affects progress in several subjects. He has lost interest in school work and has no enthusiasm for family life at the moment.

The Perma Model and Kai

Kai's family appear to provide an opportunity for family quality time, which is good, but as a teenager, he also needs activities that he can 'own'. By considering his past interests and strengths, it is possible to plan a pathway to exploring other possibilities more suited to Kai and that also help to rekindle engagement and accomplishment in school. Table 11.1 shows Kai's well-being action planning chart, which used the PERMA model to explore his options and find the right path for Kai.

Table 11.1   Kai's well-being action planning chart

	Examples drawn from the young person's experiences	Do we need to develop more opportunities in this area?	How can my child's strengths help to eliminate the gaps?
Positive emotions	E.g. we go swimming weekly as a family		
Engagement	E.g. my child does not appear to have any personal hobbies or favourite school subjects	Yes	E.g. my child is a team player – what clubs could he join?
Positive relationships	Yes, at home	He doesn't really socialise outside school	What team sports or drama clubs could he access locally or in school?
Meaning and purpose	E.g. as a family we tend to focus on our busy day-to-day routines	Maybe we could start talking about our aspirations at teatime to see what hopes we all have, no matter how small	Are there any other strengths that could help develop his sense of purpose?
Accomplishment	E.g. my child used to have merits for effort in his last school	I'll find out how his needs are being met and find out from him where he needs help	We can try to strength-spot in school and at home to build a sense of accomplishment in his life again and utilise his team working strength to provide opportunities for leading groupwork in some lessons

Finally, remember that you are the expert in your child's needs and you have the right for your voice to be heard during reviews of your child's progress. By being involved in setting goals and targets in their programmes, and reinforcing them in the home environment, you will optimise your child's learning experiences and emotional well-being.

Summary

In this chapter we have:

- explored how parents can help their child with SEND. The most important thing that a parent can do for their child is to accept them for who they are. If you are struggling in coming to terms with the impact of your child's SEND, seek emotional and practical support and knowledge;
- highlighted that parents have a key role to play in supporting the independence, competence and the inclusion of their child with SEND;
- looked at the particular responsibilities parents have in the provision of feedback regarding their child's social and emotional development;
- acknowledged the importance of parents accepting their child's growing self-determination and the benefits of allowing them to gain greater autonomy gradually.

Further Resources for Parents

Advisory Centre for Education (ACE) This is an independent registered charity which offers information about state education in England and Wales for parents of school-age children. See www.ace-ed.org.uk/

The British Psychological Society (BPS) This organisation's website includes the Directory of Chartered Psychologists. This is a searchable database that will help you to find an educational psychologist in the area where you live. See www.bps.org.uk/

Department for Education and Skills (DfES) The DfES website contains a number of links relevant to special educational needs and the services that are available. See www.dfes.gov.uk/

Educational Software Directory This site has a comprehensive list of software for different special needs. See www.educational-software-directory. net/special-needs/

Independent Panel for Special Education Advice (IPSEA) IPSEA offers free and independent legal advice and support for parents of children with special needs in England and Wales. See www.ipsea.org.uk/

Parentline This is a website that provides information to parents about special educational needs. See www.parentline.net

12
Summary

In Part 1 of this book we saw how children and young people with SEND may be at greater risk of experiencing barriers to emotional well-being than their non-disabled peers. The necessity of trying to address this issue using an interactive approach at an individual, family, peer and school/community level was emphasised.

After outlining the specific emotional issues that may arise, Positive Psychology was outlined as a paradigm for addressing the issues constructively and proactively.

Chapters 5–7 helped the practitioner to assess whether or not there are gaps in individual children's lives and what can be done proactively to support their autonomy, competence and sense of inclusion or belonging.

In Chapters 8–10 we read about a range of strategies that practitioners may use to help address the needs identified through assessment.

Recognising the important role that the parent has when actively engaged in this process, Chapter 11 offered a photocopiable summary of the general approach to supporting children's emotional well-being throughout their development.

Seligman's (2011) PERMA model was also introduced to the practitioner as it stresses the importance of positive emotions (by increasing opportunities for having fun) and identifying personal strengths (providing a platform for increasing engagement and personal meaning) as well as identifying personal goals (meaning, optimism and hope). The latter also contributes to the promotion of opportunities for self-determination. In turn, these aspects help to facilitate access to leisure and social opportunities (promoting positive relationships and social and emotional development).

It is hoped that the reader will now have at their disposal a range of knowledge and skills to actively promote the child and young person with SEND's learning and life experiences.

Finally, a flowchart summarising the approach is provided on p.136 to assist the reader in utilising the practical resources made available.

EWB/SEND Action Planning Process

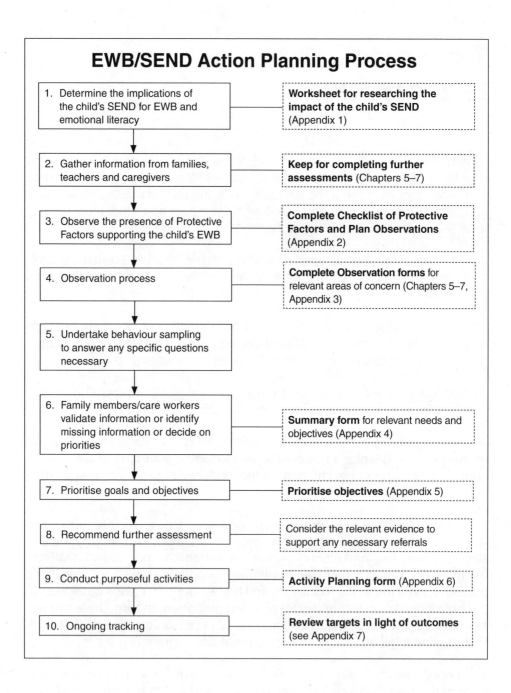

1. Determine the implications of the child's SEND for EWB and emotional literacy

Worksheet for researching the impact of the child's SEND (Appendix 1)

2. Gather information from families, teachers and caregivers

Keep for completing further assessments (Chapters 5–7)

3. Observe the presence of Protective Factors supporting the child's EWB

Complete Checklist of Protective Factors and Plan Observations (Appendix 2)

4. Observation process

Complete Observation forms for relevant areas of concern (Chapters 5–7, Appendix 3)

5. Undertake behaviour sampling to answer any specific questions necessary

6. Family members/care workers validate information or identify missing information or decide on priorities

Summary form for relevant needs and objectives (Appendix 4)

7. Prioritise goals and objectives

Prioritise objectives (Appendix 5)

8. Recommend further assessment

Consider the relevant evidence to support any necessary referrals

9. Conduct purposeful activities

Activity Planning form (Appendix 6)

10. Ongoing tracking

Review targets in light of outcomes (see Appendix 7)

Appendices

Steps 1 and 2: Barriers Worksheet

The first step towards coming to terms with a SEN or disability is to understand the implications of the SEN or disability for functioning. In turn, this may have an impact on EWB. Use the Barriers Worksheet (see Appendix 1) to record knowledge about the possible impact of a SEND.

Appendix 1: Barriers Worksheet

Name of condition/s:

Name of child:

Research sources:

Which areas of development does the SEND affect? Tick areas at risk.

Communication – understanding	Communication – expression	Communication – pragmatics (e.g. turn-taking)
Motor skills – mobility	Motor skills – fine motor control e.g. handwriting	Social skills e.g. manners, team working, play
Perception – visual	Perception – auditory	Perception – kinaesthetic
Reasoning ability – comprehension and general knowledge	Social communication e.g. shared understanding	Self-help skills e.g. toileting, dressing, organisational skills
Attention development and control	Memory	Sensory integration

What do you think may be the potential implications for the following?

	From the child's perspective	From other people's perspective
a) Learning and development		
b) Daily living		
c) Social and leisure life		

How does this affect their independence, sense of competence and belonging?

How does this affect their ability to experience positive emotions, engagement, positive relationships, meaning and accomplishment?

Step 3: Checklist of Factors Protective of EWB in CYPSEND

The next step is to complete the Checklist of Factors Protective of EWB in Children and Young People with SEND (see Appendix 2).

Emotional Well-being for Children with Special Educational Needs and Disabilities ©
Gail Bailey, 2012 (SAGE)

Appendix 2: The Checklist of Factors Protective of Emotional Well-being in Children and Young People with SEND

Section 1– Promoting the person behind the disability

This section includes items that are related to the enduring personal characteristics of the child.

Section 2 – Creating a community of caring

This section includes items related to the environmental and social characteristics surrounding the child that are supportive of adjustment.

Section 3 – Living a fulfilled life

This section includes items specifically relating to the psychological well-being of the child.

Section 4 – Physical health

This section includes factors relating to health that have a bearing on the adjustment of the child.

Section 5 – Developmental pathway

This section contains items related to change as the child develops as well as recognition that improvements in meeting needs are continually being made (e.g. as a result of technological advances).

The Checklist of Factors Supporting EWB in CYPSEND

This is a self-assessment of your current approach to supporting a young person. It will provide a solid foundation to establish the framework for action and to create a basis for target-setting and strategy development.

NAME:_____

DESIGNATION:_____

CHILD:_____

DATE: _____

SELF-ASSESSMENT

Work through the following five components of the Questionnaire. Taking each statement individually, write a score in the adjacent box based upon whether you:

TOTALLY AGREE	4
LARGELY AGREE	3
PARTLY AGREE/NOT SURE	2
LARGELY DISAGREE	1
TOTALLY DISAGREE	0

It is important that you try to be as honest as you can in order to achieve a worthwhile result.

1 PROMOTING THE PERSON BEHIND THE DISABILITY

I have been able to encourage young people with disabilities to express themselves effectively, to be assertive when required and confident enough to ask for help (see Chapters 6 and 9)

I have encouraged the self-motivation of young people to fully participate in activities of learning (see Chapters 5 and 8, 6 and 9)

I have encouraged young people to be hopeful and face the future with confidence and optimism (see Chapters 5 and 8; optimism)

I am able to help young people to become objective and help them appreciate other people's perspectives (see Chapters 7 and 10)

In the past I have helped young people to overcome barriers through problem-solving (see Chapters 6 and 9)

2 CREATING A COMMUNITY OF CARING

I have always made a concerted effort to appreciate the person rather than focus on their disability (see Chapters 5 and 8, 6 and 9)

I have been able to ensure that people surrounding the young people are both patient and sensitive to their emotional and physical needs (see Chapters 5 and 8)

I have been encouraging friends and family to spend 'quality time' with the young person to foster a sense of security and belonging (see Chapters 7 and 10)

I do not make assumptions about how to help a young person with a disability. Rather I work with an individual to discover their needs (see Chapters 6 and 9)

I have changed the attitude of the family to become positive (if necessary) and generate hope for the future (see Chapters 7 and 10; optimism)

3 LIVING A FULFILLED LIFE

I have made a tangible difference in the daily life of a young person living with a disability by promoting their sense of independence (see Chapters 5 and 8)

In the past I have boosted the young person's morale by helping them to engage with their work, which enabled them to keep pace with their peers (see Chapters 6 and 9)

I have taken active steps to ensure that the young person has a sense of belonging by ensuring that professional and support people are both good role models and take the trouble to be inclusive (see Chapters 7 and 10)

I have taken steps to ensure that the young person can recognise and make the most of their personal strengths (see Chapters 6 and 9)

Through my work I have encouraged the young person to be more optimistic (see Chapters 5 and 8)

4 PHYSICAL HEALTH

I have employed a structured approach to help the young person fully understand the implications of their condition on their physical functioning and emotional health (see Chapters 6 and 9, 7 and 10)

I have consulted with other professionals to determine whether the condition is stable or not and fully understand the implications (see Chapters 6 and 9)

I fully appreciate not only the prime disability but also other health conditions that may impact upon their well-being (see Chapters 6 and 9)

I have ensured that family and friends are aware that the young person needs sufficient rest to ensure that fatigue does not impact on their behaviour (see the Health section in Chapter 5 – this impacts on all factors supporting EWB)

I have ensured that the daily routine of the young person contains an active element for physical exercise to overcome anxiety (see Chapters 5–10)

5 DEVELOPMENT PATHWAY

I have created a Plan–Do–Check–Act routine to review the young person's progress in the light of their development and disability (see Chapters 6 and 9)

I ensure that as part of my own professional development I am up to date with technological aids that can overcome emotional and disability barriers to the full participation of young people (as this has a potential impact on independence, capability and belonging) (see Chapters 5 and 8)

I ensure that I take active measures to keep up to date with medical advances that may contribute solutions towards the management of the disability (see Chapters 5 and 8)

I make an effort to look for interests that excite young people so that I can build real opportunities for active engagement and the pleasure of accomplishment (see Chapters 5 and 8)

I have nurtured young people to acquire new skills so that they can enhance their ability to participate fully in learning and leisure (see Chapters 5–10)

When you have completed this assessment, score each section and circle those that score 2 or less. You can find more information, including strategies on how to improve the situation for the child, by turning to the chapters noted in brackets.

Steps 4–6: Observation and Validation

The next step is to undertake a comprehensive observation process. Chapters 5–7 include assessments of autonomy (My support), hope (My goals), Health, competence (My capabilities) and connectedness (Towards belonging). Use the Observation Worksheet (see Appendix 3) to help you.

Further behaviour sampling may also be necessary. This means finding out more about events leading up to a behaviour giving cause for concern, identifying the particular behaviour to target and the consequences of the behaviour as it stands. For example, a child with ASD who is sensitive to sound may cope well with settling into a new school routine except for lunchtimes when there is a lot of noise in the canteen and then may be very unsettled for the rest of the day. Such sampling can help identify the measures to put in place (e.g. Social Stories) to help them anticipate the noisy atmosphere and apply coping strategies to help them remain calm, and to manage their emotional responses. It is also good practice to validate all your observations with family members and/or careworkers, to ensure that you have identified all relevant factors, needs and objectives, and any missing information. You can use the Summary Form (see Appendix 4) to help you in this task. Now you are fully prepared to move to the next step, deciding on priorities and/or seeking further referrals.

Emotional Well-being for Children with Special Educational Needs and Disabilities ©
Gail Bailey, 2012 (SAGE)

Appendix 3: Observation Worksheet

Use this sheet to make notes about your observations or the comments of other adults or children and to summarise issues for attention.

Section of checklist	Direct observations (label DO) or observations from others (e.g. child (label CO), parents (label PO), teaching assistants (label TO))	Needs and objectives identified as requiring action according to the items assessed in Chapters 5–7 (tick item requiring attention)
A. Autonomy – towards independence		A1 A2 A3 A4 A5 A6
B. Belonging – towards effective relationships and social inclusion		B1 B2 B3 B4 B5 B6
C. Competence – towards keeping pace with peers		C1 C2 C3 C4 C5 C6 C7 C8

O. Factors supporting systemic optimism		O1 O2 O3 O4
H. Physical factors influencing adjustment		H1 H2 H3 H4 H5

Appendix 4: Summary Form

Needs	Objectives
Autonomy –	Autonomy –
Competence –	Competence –
Belonging –	Belonging –

Steps 7 and 8: Prioritising Objectives and/or Seeking Referrals

Now that you have completed the observation process you can prioritise your goals and objectives. Use the Prioritise Objectives Form (see Appendix 5) to help you. You are also in a better position to consider relevant resources for support or to seek additional referrals, if these are necessary.

Appendix 5: Prioritise Objectives Form

Needs	Main objective
Autonomy –	
Competence –	
Belonging –	

Step 9: Purposeful Activities

There may be several activities you can undertake to meet your goals and objectives. Using a Weekly Activity Planning Form (see Appendix 6) is a good place to start.

Chapters 8–10 provide examples of strategies that can promote emotional well-being. Worksheets are provided in the Appendices to help you. Weekly Strengths Diaries (see Appendices 8 and 9) are an excellent way of supporting a child with SEND, in both identifying and reinforcing strengths and using strengths to solve problems and set goals. The My STEP Forward Worksheet (see Appendix 10) and the Well-being Action Planning Chart using the PERMA model (see Appendix 11) are also reproduced there.

 Emotional Well-being for Children with Special Educational Needs and Disabilities © Gail Bailey, 2012 (SAGE)

Appendix 6: Weekly Activity Planning Form

Needs	Day of week and activity
Autonomy –	
Competence –	
Belonging –	

Step 10: Tracking Progress

It is essential that you continually monitor progress throughout your involvement with a child with SEND. Reviewing all the forms and worksheets you have completed at regular intervals will enable you to keep progress on target. You can also use them to help you to review objectives and goals in light of assessment outcomes. Use the Tracking Progress Form (see Appendix 7) to monitor and record objectives, activities and the child's response and progress. This is a particularly valuable resource for future planning.

Emotional Well-being for Children with Special Educational Needs and Disabilities ©
Gail Bailey, 2012 (SAGE)

Appendix 7: Tracking Progress Form

Objective and activity	Response and outcome
Autonomy – WEEK 1 WEEK 2 WEEK 3 WEEK 4	
Competence – WEEK 1 WEEK 2 WEEK 3 WEEK 4	
Belonging – WEEK 1 WEEK 2 WEEK 3 WEEK 4	

Emotional Well-being for Children with Special Educational Needs and Disabilities ©
Gail Bailey, 2012 (SAGE)

Appendix 8: Weekly Strengths Diary 1

NAME:

My Top Strengths are:

1

2

3

4

5

Day of week	How did I use my strength?
Monday	
Tuesday	
Wednesday	
Thursday	
Friday	
Saturday	
Sunday	

Which strength did I use the most often?

Which strength made me feel the most energised?

Which strength helped me or others the most?

Appendix 9: Weekly Strengths Diary 2: Problem-solving and Goal-setting

NAME:

My Top Strengths were:

1

2

3

4

5

This week I am going to try to use my strengths in new ways to help with challenges.

Day of week	How did I use my strength in a new way?
Monday	
Tuesday	
Wednesday	
Thursday	
Friday	
Saturday	
Sunday	

Appendix 10: My STEP Forward Worksheet

Sense
Try to understand
Energise
Push forward

Think/talk through/record your ideas for sorting out a problem you may have.

See example in Figure 10.1.

Appendix 11: Well-being Action Planning Chart Using The PERMA Model

	Examples drawn from young person's experience	Is there a gap that threatens EWB?	How can the signature strengths help eliminate the gaps?
Positive emotions			
Engagement			
Positive relationships			
Meaning and purpose			
Accomplishment			

The PERMA Model is described in more detail in Seligman, 2011.

 Emotional Well-being for Children with Special Educational Needs and Disabilities © Gail Bailey, 2012 (SAGE)

Bibliography

ABRAMSON, L.Y., METALSKY, G. and ALLOY, L.B. (1987) The helplessness theory of depression: does the research test the theory? In L.Y. ABRAMSON (ed.), *Social Cognition and Clinical Psychology: A Synthesis*. New York: Guilford Press.

ABRAMSON, L.Y., SELIGMAN, M.E. and TEASDALE, J. (1978) Learned helplessness in humans: critique and re-formulation. *Journal of Abnormal Psychology*, 87, 49–74.

AINSCOW, M. (1995) Education for all: making it happen. *Support for Learning*, 10(4), 147–54.

ALBRECHT, G.L. and DEVLIEGER, P.J. (1999) The disability paradox: high quality of life against all odds. *Social Science and Medicine*, 48, 977–88.

ALDWIN, C.M. and SUTTON, K.J. (1998) A developmental perspective on post-traumatic growth. In R.G. TEDESCHI and L.G. CALHOUN (eds), *Post-Traumatic Growth: Positive Changes in the Aftermath of Crisis*. Mahwah, NJ: Lawrence Erlbaum Associates, pp. 43–63.

BAILEY, G. (2011) A positive exploration of the emotional well-being of children and young people with visual impairments. Unpublished doctoral thesis, University College London.

BANDURA, A. (1977) Self-efficacy: toward a unifying theory of behavioural change. *Psychological Review*, 84, 191–215.

BANERJEE, R., DAINES, R. and WATLING, D. (2004) *The Children's Social Behaviour Project: A Research-based Emotional Literacy Curriculum for Key Stage 2 A.E.P.* Course presentation and documentation, November.

CAMERON, R.J. and MAGINN, C. (2009) *Achieving Positive Outcomes for Children in Care*. London: Sage.

CHEAVENS, J.S., FELDMAN, D.B., GUM, A., SCOTT, T.M. and SNYDER, C.R. (2006) Hope therapy in a community sample: a pilot investigation. *Social Indicators Research*, 77, 61–8.

Code of Practice on the Identification and Assessment of Special Educational Needs (1994) Department for Education. London: HMSO.

DAHLSGAARD, K. (2003) *Children's Strength Survey* in M.E.P. Seligman, *Authentic Happiness: Using the New Positive Psychology to Realize Your Potential for Lasting Fulfillment*. London: Nicholas Brearley. pp. 232–44.

DANIELS, H. (2001) *Vygotsky and Pedagogy*. London: Routledge/Falmer.

DAVIS, P. (2003) *Including Children with Visual Impairments in Mainstream Schools: A Practical Guide*. London: David Fulton.

Department for Children Schools and Families (DCSF) (2008) *SEAL Resource: Introductory Booklet*. London: Stationary Office. (Available as a downloadable PDF file from www.bandapilot.org.uk/secondary) Also explore SEAL webpages of DCSF website.

DELLE FAVE, A. and MASSIMINI, F. (2003) Making disability into a resource. *The Psychologist*, 16(3), 133–4.

DEPARTMENT FOR EMPLOYMENT AND SKILLS (DES) (1989) *Assessment and Statements of SEN: procedures within the education, health and social services*. Circular 22/89. London: HMSO.

DEPARTMENT OF HEALTH (DoH) (2009) *Overarching Report of Findings from the Adult Autism Strategy Consultation Activities*. Prepared for the Central Office for Information and the Department of Health by Opinion Leader. London: DoH.

DIENER, E. (2000) Subjective well-being: the science of happiness and a proposal for a national index. *American Psychologist*, 55, 34–43.

The DISABILITY DISCRIMINATION ACT (2005) QE II Parliament. London: The Stationery Office.

DODDS, A.G., BAILEY, P., PEARSON, A. and YATES, L. (1991) Psychological factors in acquired visual impairment: the development of a scale of adjustment. *Journal of Visual Impairment and Blindness*, 85, 306–10.

DOSS, B. and HATCHER, B. (1996) Self-determination as a family affair: parents' perspectives on self-determination. In D.J. SANDS and M.L. WEHMEYER (eds), *Self-determination across the Lifespan: Independence and Choice for People with Disabilities*. Baltimore, MD: Paul H. Brookes, pp. 51–63.

DWECK, C.S. (2000) *Self-theories: Their Role in Motivation, Personality and Development*. Philadelphia, PA: Taylor and Francis.

The Education Act (1944) Board of Education White Paper *Educational Reconstruction* Cmd. 6458. London: HMSO. Retrieved online 1 March 2012 at http://www.educationengland.org.uk/documents/pdfs/1943-educational-reconstruction.pdf

ELLIOT, T.R., KURYLO, M. and RIVERA, P. (2002) Positive growth following acquired physical disability. In C.R. SNYDER and S.J. LOPEZ (eds), *Handbook of Positive Psychology*. New York: Oxford University Press, Chapter 50.

EMERSON, E. (2007) *The Mental Health of Children and Adolescents with Learning Disabilities in Britain*. London: The Mental Health Foundation.

FAUPEL, A., HERRICK, E. and SHARP, P. (1998) *Anger Management: A Practical Guide*. London: Fulton.

FAUPEL, A.(ed) (2003) *Emotional Literacy Guidelines*. Southampton City Council.

FIGUERIDO, J.M. and FRANK, J.D. (1982) Subjective independence: the clinical hallmark of demoralisation. *Archives of General Psychiatry*, 23, 353–63.

FREDERICKSON, N. and CLINE, T. (2009) *Special Educational Needs, Inclusion and Diversity: A Textbook* (2nd edition). Buckingham: Open University Press.

FREDERICKSON, N., WARREN, L. and TURNER, J. (2005) 'Circle of Friends': an exploration of impact over time. *Educational Psychology in Practice*, 21, 197–217.

FREDERICKSON, N., WEBSTER, A. and WRIGHT, A. (1991) Psychological assessment: a change in emphasis. *Educational Psychology in Practice*, 6(5), 23–32.

GRAY, C. (2000) *New Social Story Book*. London: Future Horizons.

HUGO, V. (1877) *Histoire d'un Crime*. Translated by T.H. Joyce and Arthur Locker. Available as an e-book online at Project Guttenberg: www.gutenberg.org/ebooks/10381

HUPPERT, F., BAYLIS, N. and KEVERNE, B. (2004) The science of well-being. *The Psychologist*, 17(1), 6–7.

HUPPERT, F.L. and SO, T. (2009) What percentage of people in Europe are flourishing and what characterizes them? Paper presented at the First World Congress on Positive Psychology, Philadelphia, June 18–21.

LEACH, C.J.C., GREEN, S.L. and GRANT, A.M. (2011) Flourishing youth provision: the potential role of positive psychology and coaching in enhancing youth services. *International Journal of Evidence-Based Coaching and Mentoring*, 9(1), 44–58.

LING, J. (2010) *I Can't Do That: My Social Stories to Help with Communication, Self-care and Social Skills*. London: Sage.

LINKOWSKI, D.C. (1967) A study of the relationship between acceptance of disability and response to rehabilitation. Unpublished doctoral dissertation, State University of New York at Buffalo, NY.

LINKOWSKI, D.C. (1971) A scale to measure acceptance of disability. *Rehabilitation Counselling Bulletin*, 14, 236–44.

LINKOWSKI, D.C. (1987) *The Acceptance of Disability Scale: Advances in Psychosocial Rehabilitation*. A report on current rehabilitation at the George Washington University Medical Center. Washington, DC: Rehabilitation Research and Training Center, Dept. of Psychiatry and Behavioral Sciences, George Washington University Medical Center.

LINLEY, P.A. (2000) The example of trauma. *The Psychologist*, 13(7), 353–5.

LINLEY, P.A. and JOSEPH, S. (2003) Trauma and personal growth. *The Psychologist*, 16(3), 135.

McCORMACK, G. (2011) *In the Driving Seat: A Toolkit*. Wigan: Positive Eye Ltd.

MILLER, A., FERGUSON, E. and BYRNE, I. (2000) Pupils' causal attributions for difficult classroom behaviour. *British Journal of Educational Psychology*, 70, 85–96.

NEWMAN, T. and BLACKBURN, S. (2002) *Interchange 78. Transitions in the Lives of Young People: Resilience Factors*. Barnardo's Policy, Research and Influencing Unit. London: Barnardo's.

OFFICE FOR NATIONAL STATISTICS (ONS) (1999) *Mental Health of Children and Adolescents*. ONS (99) 409. London: Government Statistical Service.

PETERSON, C. and SELIGMAN, M.R.P. (2004). *Character Strengths and Virtues: A Handbook and Classification*. Washington, DC: APA Press.

RAE, T. (2000) *Confidence, Assertiveness and Self-esteem: A Series of 12 Sessions for Secondary School Students*. Bristol: Lucky Duck Publications.

RAE, T. (2007) *Dealing with Feelings: An Emotional Literacy Curriculum for Children Aged 7–13*. London: Sage.

RASMUSSEN, H.N., NEUFELD, J.E., BOUWKAMP, L.E., EDWARDS, L.M., ITO, A., MAGYAR-MOE, J.L., RYDER, J.A. and LOPEZ, S.J. (2003) Environmental assessment: examining influences on optimal human functioning. In S.J. LOPEZ and C.R. SNYDER (eds), *Positive Psychological Assessment: A Handbook of Models and Measures*. Washington, DC: American Psychological Association, Chapter 28.

RUSSELL, P. (2008) *Aiming High! Support for Parents of Disabled Children and Young People*. Paper presented at Leading Edge Psychology Day Conference: Parenting Today: Bringing Up Children in Challenging Times. University College London, 31 March.

RUTTER, M. (1987) Psycho-social resilience and protective mechanisms. *American Journal of Orthopsychiatry*, 57, 316–31.

RYAN, R.M. and DECI, E.L. (2000) Self-determination theory and the facilitation of intrinsic motivation, social development and well-being. *American Psychologist*, 55, 68–77.

SALOVEY, P. and SLUYTER, D.J. (1997) *Emotional Development and Emotional Intelligence: Educational Implications*. New York: Basic Books.

SELIGMAN, M.E.P. (1975) *Helplessness: On Depression, Development and Death*. San Francisco: Freedman.

SELIGMAN, M.E.P. (2003) *Authentic Happiness: Using the New Positive Psychology to Realize Your Potential for Lasting Fulfilment*. London: Nicholas Brearley.

SELIGMAN, M.E.P. (2011) *Flourish: A New Understanding of Happiness and Well-being and How To Achieve Them*. London: Nicholas Brearley.

SELIGMAN, M.E.P. and CSIKSZENTMIHALYI, M. (2000) Positive psychology: an introduction. *American Psychologist*, 55, 5–14.

SHOTTON, G. (2009) *Pupil-friendly IEPs, Target Sheets and Other Pupil-friendly Resources*. London: Sage/Lucky Duck Publications.

SIN, N.L. and LYUBORMIRSKY, S. (2009) Enhancing well-being and alleviating depressive symptoms with positive psychology interventions: a practice-friendly meta-analysis. *Journal of Clinical Psychology*, 65(5), 467–87.

SNYDER, C.R., HOZA, B., PELHAM, W.E., RAPOFF, M., WARE, L., DANOVSKY, M., et al. (1997) The development and validation of the children's hope scale. *Journal of Pediatric Psychology*, 22(3), 399–421.

SOLITY, J. (1993) Assessment through teaching: a case of mistaken identity. *Educational and Child Psychology*, 10(4), 27–47.

STEELE, C. (2000) The importance of positive self image and group image. Paper presented at the Positive Psychology Summit, Washington, DC, October.

TEDESCHI, R.G., PARK, C.L. and CALHOUN, L.G. (1998) Post-traumatic growth: conceptual issues. In R.G. TEDESCHI and L.G. CALHOUN (eds), *Post-Traumatic Growth: Positive Changes in the Aftermath of Crisis*. Mahwah, NJ: Lawrence Erlbaum Associates, pp. 1–21.

UN Convention on the Rights of the Child (1989). Geneva: United Nations.

VYGOTSKY, L.S. (1987) *The Collected Works of L.S. Vygotsky. Vol. 2: The Fundamentals of Defectology (Abnormal Psychology and Learning Disabilities)*. New York: Plenum Press.

WAG (Welsh Assembly Government) (2001) *Everybody's Business: Welsh Assembly Government Strategy Document on Child and Adolescent Mental Health Services*. Cardiff: Welsh Assembly Government.

WAG (Welsh Assembly Government) (2010) *Thinking Positively*. Cardiff: Welsh Assembly Government.

WEARE, K. (2004) *Developing the Emotionally Literate School*. London: Sage.

WEINER, B. (1979) A theory of motivation for some classroom experiences. *Journal of Educational Psychology*, 71, 3–25.

WEINER, B. (1985) An attributional theory of achievement motivation and emotion. *Psychological Review*, 92, 548–73.

WILSON, S. (2003) *Disability, Counselling and Psychotherapy: Challenges and Opportunities*. Basingstoke: Palgrave/Macmillan.

WORLD HEALTH ORGANISATION (2001) *International Classification of Functioning, Disability and Health*. Geneva: WHO. Retrieved March 8 2002 from www.who.int/icidh.

WRIGHT, B. and LOPEZ, S.J. (2002) Widening the diagnostic focus: a case for including human strengths and environmental resources. In C.R. SNYDER and S.J. LOPEZ (eds), *The Handbook of Positive Psychology*. New York: Oxford University Press, pp. 26–44.

Websites

Contact A Family (CAF): www.cafamily.org.uk

Centre for Applied Positive Psychology (CAPP): www.cappeu.com

Center for Non-violent Communication: www.cnvc.org

Children's Relationships, Emotions and Social Skills (CRESS), at the University of Sussex): www.sussex.ac.uk/Users/robinb/

Inclusive Solutions: www.inclusive-solutions.com (re Circle of Friends)

Kidscape: www.kidscape.org.uk

Mental Health Foundation: www.mentalhealth.org.uk

Positive Eye: www.positiveeye.co.uk

Index

Added to a page number 'f' denotes a figure and 't' denotes a table.

SPECIAL EDUCATIONAL NEEDS

A Guide for Inclusive Practice

Edited by **Lindsay Peer** and **Gavin Reid** *both Educational Psychologists*

'This book is timely. I hope that it will be very widely read' -Mary Warnock

With a Foreword from Baroness Mary Warnock, this book provides a comprehensive overview of the field of special educational needs (SEN). It contains chapters written by a range of experts on different aspects of SEN, and is full of practical suggestions for how to achieve effective, inclusive practice. Various research perspectives are considered, the value of labels is examined and the need to recognize the overlapping characteristics between different syndromes is highlighted. Chapters focus on translating theory into classroom practice, and include case studies covering the Birth to 19 age range.

There is coverage of:

- SEN and the state of research
- SEN and legal issues
- parents' perspectives
- Speech and language difficulties
- Dyspraxia and occupational therapy
- Dyslexia
- Dyscalculia

- Auditory Processing Disorder
- Behavioural Optometry
- Attention Deficit Hyperactivity Disorder (ADHD)
- Asperger Syndrome and Autistic Spectrum Disorder
- Tourette Syndrome

Ideal for those undertaking teacher education courses, as well as experienced teachers, therapists and policy makers, this book is a guide to understanding and supporting learners with additional needs.

READERSHIP

Those undertaking teacher education courses, as well as experienced teachers, therapists and policy makers

2011 • 328 pages
Cloth (978-0-85702-162-5) • £70.00
Paper (978-0-85702-163-2) • £23.99

ALSO FROM SAGE

PARTNERSHIP WORKING TO SUPPORT SPECIAL EDUCATIONAL NEEDS & DISABILITIES

Rona Tutt *Consultant, writer, researcher and former President of NAHT*

In order to achieve the best outcomes for all children and young people, schools must work in partnership with students, parents, other professionals and the wider community. In this changing landscape of education, the notion of the traditional school is fast disappearing. This book looks at what is possible in this exciting new world, and how some teachers and other professionals are putting into practice the best principles of multi-agency working.

Finding innovative ways of supporting children and young people with special educational needs and disabilities (SEND) in this context is more important than ever, as children are being diagnosed with increasingly complex needs. Those working with children need to be aware of the fresh opportunities that are opening up and which can help every individual to maximise their full potential. This book examines how partnership working affects children with SEND and is filled with case studies of effective practice from real schools and services. It is a must-have for those looking at how to work together to achieve positive outcomes for all.

READERSHIP

SENCOs, school leaders and teaching assistants working with children of any age

2010 • 144 pages
Cloth (978-0-85702-147-2) • £63.00
Paper (978-0-85702-148-9) • £20.99

ALSO FROM SAGE